advanced that Sterne had established *Tristam Shandy* as fiction by the time he had written half of it.

The last chapter first examines a series of events unintentionally brought about by Uncle Toby, which Tristram credits with having made him the kind of writer and person that he is. This series, or sequence, of events overlaps that of Walter and Tristram. It begins in the first volume and ends in the sixth. Attention is then called to other sequences of events, and a scheme is presented of the parts that make up the whole of *Tristram Shandy*. The study of the novel is concluded by examining the words of Yorick, with which the book closes. The speaker, who is a great deal like Sterne himself and who has been made increasingly important in the latter portion of the book, makes a statement about what kind of work has been written and how valuable it is. The final conclusion is that *Tristram Shandy*, although primarily and preponderantly a work of fiction, ultimately reveals, and is a most important part of, the life of Sterne — man, minister, and novelist.

STUDIES IN ENGLISH LITERATURE

Volume XXII

THE RELATION OF
TRISTRAM SHANDY
TO THE LIFE OF STERNE

by

OVERTON PHILIP JAMES

Northeast Louisiana State College

1966

MOUTON & CO.

THE HAGUE · PARIS

© Copyright 1966 by Mouton & Co., Publishers, The Hague,
The Netherlands.

*No part of this book may be translated or reproduced in any form,
by print, photoprint, microfilm, or any other means, without written
permission from the publishers.*

Printed in The Netherlands by Mouton & Co., Printers, The Hague

ACKNOWLEDGEMENTS

During the course of this study of Tristram Shandy and Laurence Sterne, I have been graciously assisted, first of all, by Professor John M. Aden of Vanderbilt, who made me aware of certain controlling questions and afforded me constructive criticism and wise counsel. Professor Edgar Duncan has read the manuscript and made invaluable suggestions. And Mrs. Edith Megling has painstakingly typed it for me.

I am also grateful to President Cecil Humphreys of Memphis State University and to the Chairman of the English Department, Dr. H. B. Evans, of the same institution, for several reasons.

My wife, Nola, has been a most important part of this work. Without her confidence I would not have begun it, and without her encouragement I would not have completed it. In the meantime our son, Joe, has waited patiently.

TABLE OF CONTENTS

Acknowledgements 5

Preface 9

I. The Author and his Work: The Problem and the Scholarship 11

II. The Man and the Novelist 32

III. The Minister and the Novelist 56

IV. The Transition from Minister to Novelist 79

V. The Novel: From the Beginning to the Birth and the Misnaming of Tristram Shandy 102

VI. The Novel: From the Beginning to the Final Comment of Yorick 129

Conclusion 162

Bibliography 165

PREFACE

Tristram Shandy wrote of the way his father argued the importance of names: "Like all systematick reasoners, he would move both heaven and earth, and twist and torture every thing in nature to support his hypothesis. In a word, I repeat it over again; – he was serious." Since caution must be exercised – if Walter Shandy's error is to be avoided – in coming to serious conclusions about "The Life and Opinions of Tristram Shandy, Gentleman", I have, first of all, examined the course of Sterne criticism. And I have noticed particularly whether and for what reason Sterne's work has been called "biography" or "fiction". Although the question might appear to be one which would have delighted Walter Shandy, a proper evaluation of the work depends to a great extent on whether, or to what degree, *Tristram Shandy* is biography or fiction.

In the first chapter of this study I have observed that Sterne critics, until about thirty years ago, generally agreed that *Tristram Shandy* was autobiographical, but that later ones have tended to separate the man from his work and to treat it as a product of his imagination. Depending in part on a hundred and fifty years of biographical criticism and on thirty of "New Criticism", I have argued that the following view of the matter will help to understand and evaluate the man and his work: Although *Tristram Shandy* was the imaginative work of Laurence Sterne, nevertheless it owed much to the kind of life the author lived, and what he came to be depended on his having written it.

After examining in the second and third chapters of this paper the life and ministry of Sterne, insofar as they could be separated,

I have concluded, despite Tristram's warning, that some of the serious elements in Sterne's life were partly responsible for *Tristram Shandy's* being other than another jest book. Although Sterne's formal education and his reading and his years of being a minister cannot be given credit for the unique kind of imagination and humor which the work exhibits, they were responsible for a good part of its contents, composition, and meaning.

In the fourth chapter I have closely examined the presentation of Yorick, which is set apart from what follows it by two black pages. Sterne appears to have modeled the character of Yorick in part after his own. I have found reason to believe that he presented the life and death of Yorick in order to remove himself from the novel and to leave Tristram to write in character.

The fifth chapter has been devoted to examining the first portion of the novel, which ends with "MY FATHER'S LAMENTATIONS" at the middle of the fourth volume. This part contains the reciprocally creative efforts of Tristram and his father. The father tries to bring into the world an excellent son; the son tries to present in the novel his father, his father's disappointments, and himself as the chief disappointment.

In the last chapter I have first examined a series of events unintentionally brought about by Uncle Toby that Tristram credits with having made him the kind of person and writer that he is. This series, or sequence, of events overlaps that of Walter and Tristram. It begins in the first volume and ends in the sixth. I have next called attention to other sequences of events, and I have presented a scheme of the parts that make up the whole of *Tristram Shandy*. Finally, I have concluded the study of the relation of the man and the minister to the novelist and the novel by examining the words of Yorick, with which the book closes. The speaker, who is a great deal like Sterne himself, makes a statement about what kind of work has been written and how valuable it is.

I

THE AUTHOR AND HIS WORK: THE PROBLEM AND THE SCHOLARSHIP

For over a hundred and fifty years following its publication, *The Life and Opinions of Tristram Shandy, Gentleman* was generally regarded as the life and opinions of Laurence Sterne, Prebendary of York. Tristram Shandy's whimsical nature with its touch, or smear, of evil was thought to be a revelation of Sterne's. It was likewise believed that the details of Sterne's life coincided with what the novel revealed: His father, Roger Sterne, bequeathed little more to his son than impulsiveness and improvidence. Laurence's mother, the sutler's daughter, gave to and elicited from her son a good share of her own grossness. It was also believed that his education instead of correcting his whimsy confirmed it: While he was attending a public school notorious for its laxness, his most remarkable achievement was writing his name on the ceiling. His four years at Cambridge were spent in dawdling, in learning to dislike scholasticism (which might have disciplined his thinking), and in finding a sanction for dislike of scholasticism in John Locke's *Essay Concerning Human Understanding*. His capricious friend, John Hall-Stevenson, was credited with further abetting Sterne's talent for whimsy by making his library, stocked with *facetiae*, available to him and by making him a member of the Demoniacs of Crazy Castle. It was believed that Sterne did not take his ministerial duties seriously enough. If on his way to church Sterne happened to flush a covey of birds, he would leave his congregation waiting. And his failing to secure ecclesiastical preferment was attributed to his toying with his uncle Jacques Sterne's mistress. His changing from minister to novelist was believed to be another example of his whimsical nature. A more resolute person would have stayed with one profession, or, at least, would have changed earlier. Sterne, however, late in life turned from the ministry to novel writing. He produced, as he naturally would, a masterpiece of disorder. Finally, like Yorick, whose name he had taken, Sterne could not stay buried, but was dug up again by bodysnatchers for medical students to "examine too curiously".

Only since the beginning of the second quarter of the twentieth century has the general opinion of Sterne and his work begun to change. Probably, the change can be attributed in part to the fact that literary criticism about the same time began to separate the life of an author from his literary creations.[1] Since then it has become less certain that Sterne's life was the subject of his novel. Although recent critics have come to deny the identity of Laurence Sterne and Tristram Shandy,[2] the habit of biographical interpretation has been hard to break, and in this case the reasons for breaking it have not gained much attention.[3]

It might well be that Sterne himself was partly responsible for the reader's identifying him with Tristram. In some of his letters he called himself "Tristram", or "Shandy"; and once or twice

---

[1] Meyer H. Abrams in *The Mirror and the Lamp* (New York, Oxford University Press, 1935), pp. 26-39, summarizes the rise of objective criticism, and marks its beginning in the middle twenties with the writings of I. A. Richards, T. S. Eliot, and John Crowe Ransom. See also William K. Wimsatt, Jr. and Cleanth Brooks, *Literary Criticism: A Short History* (New York, Alfred A. Knopf, 1957), pp. 731 f. Brooks and Wimsatt attribute the spread of objective criticism to the "relatively new kind of graduate school study that seeks to substitute for the poem not the author ... but the audience".

[2] Rufus D. Putney, "Apostle of Laughter", in *Age of Johnson: Essays Presented to Chauncey Brewster Tinker* (New Haven, Yale University Press, 1949), p. 162, credits Edwin Muir with having demonstrated in 1929 that Tristram was not Sterne. I have been unable to locate the work by Muir.

[3] Implications that Tristram and Sterne were much alike are still being expressed. See: Wilbur L. Cross, *The Life and Times of Laurence Sterne*, 3d ed. rev. (New Haven, Yale University Press, 1929); James Aiken Work's "Introduction", to *The Life and Opinions of Tristram Shandy, Gentleman* (New York, Odyssey Press, 1940); Lodwick Hartley, *This is Lorence* (Chapel Hill, University of North Carolina Press, 1943); and Peter Quennell, *Four Portraits* (London, William Collins, 1945), in the U.S.: *The Profane Virtues* (New York, Viking Press, 1945).

in the novel he identified Tristram with himself. Although few, the instances were sufficient to cause Sterne and Tristram to be identified for all of the novel.[4] It is also probable that Sterne's having Tristram be both narrator and hero contributed to the confusion. Generally, readers have some difficulty in separating an author from his chief character, and more difficulty in distinguishing between the author and his narrator. And whenever, as in the case of *Tristram Shandy*, the main character and the narrator are the same, they often are unable to distinguish between the writer and his persona. It is possible that the early critics of Sterne had difficulty in separating Sterne from *Tristram Shandy* because Tristram performed this dual role.

It might also be said in extenuation of the earlier critics of *Tristram Shandy* that a complete separation of Sterne from his work would have been impossible. Although Tristram Shandy and Laurence Sterne are not the same, there is, nevertheless, a causal relationship between them. Sterne's life did not lead to his writing the book; biography cannot explain literary creativity.[5] On the other hand, it seems reasonable to hold that if Laurence Sterne had lived a different kind of life, he would have written *Tristram Shandy* differently, if he had written it at all. The converse appears equally reasonable: *Tristram Shandy* made possible the writing of *A Sentimental Journey*; and two successful literary ventures must have made Sterne's life different from what it otherwise would have been.

It is hoped that an insistence on the causal relationship between Sterne and his work – that although Tristram cannot be identified with Sterne, the conditions in Sterne's life affected the way the novel was written – will have at least a small part in offsetting the injustice done to man and novel by the long-continued identification of Sterne and Tristram and by the recent tendency to neglect Sterne the author. Because Sterne had Tristram begin the

---

[4] Alan B. Howes, *Yorick and the Critics: Sterne's Reputation in England, 1760-1868* (New Haven, Yale University Press, 1958), p. 5, n. 7.
[5] In *SRL* (January 20, 1940), p. 17, Alexander Cowie protested that W. B. C. Watkins had used biography to explain the creativity of Swift, Johnson, and Sterne in *Perilous Balance: The Tragic Genius of Swift, and Sterne* (Princeton, Princeton University Press, 1939).

novel by relating the begetting of the narrator-hero, and because Tristram continued to deal with sex even to the end of the cock-and-bull story, Sterne himself was called "Smutty Sterne".[6] Because Sterne fashioned a Tristram who wept easily and described other characters who wept still more easily, Sterne was called "sentimental".[7] Although recent investigations have begun to make doubtful that the facts of Sterne's life warranted his being called either smutty or sentimental, the injustice was done more to the man than to the author.

It would seem that the method of arriving at the condemnation of Sterne the man would have hindered recognition of Sterne the artist and of *Tristram Shandy* as a work of art. It is difficult to see how Sterne could have been regarded as a creative artist instead of a journalist when the life and opinions of Tristram Shandy were believed to be those of Laurence Sterne. It is equally difficult to see how *Tristram Shandy* could have been regarded as an imaginative construct instead of a journal. But despite the conclusions to which the identification of Sterne and his work led, he continued to be called a "novelist" and his work continued to be called a "novel". Although it is puzzling how they could have been so regarded in the face of the identification, it must be admitted that they received a certain amount of fair treatment. It was, however, not enough. The identification too long delayed the investigation of Sterne as a creative artist and of *Tristram Shandy* as a product of creative artistry.[8]

A few examples will perhaps serve as an index of the damaging effect of the circular reasoning about *Tristram Shandy*. Because the book dealt with prurient matters, Sterne was smutty minded;

---

[6] Howes, *op. cit.*, p. 7, n. 5, asserts that little verification can be found for Dr. Johnson's calling Sterne "*licentious* and *dissolute* in conversation". Howes also states that Dr. Johnson's assessment of Sterne's character has long been regarded as most damaging.

[7] Ernest Dilworth in *The Unsentimental Journey of Laurence Sterne* (New York, King's Crown Press, 1948), argues the case for the lack of mawkish emotionalism in *Tristram Shandy* as well as in *A Sentimental Journey*.

[8] Herbert Read in *The Sense of Glory* (New York, Harcourt Brace and Company, 1930), pp. 126 f., argued that Sterne's being accepted as a popular writer precluded "the need to explain his achievement".

because Sterne was smutty minded, *Tristram Shandy* dealt with prurient matters. The beginning, middle, and end of the book was seen as the author's stepping into filth, wading across it, and wiping his feet at the end of the journey. It was filth for filth's sake. Praise or blame for the author revolved about whether or not the filth was offensive. The question was long debated in a way that would have delighted Walter Shandy: Thackeray called it the "impure presence";[9] Saintsbury directed attention to Sterne's remark about the child's playing on the floor, showing "a good deal that is usually concealed";[10] and Virginia Woolf denounced the self-righteous Victorians, who were offended by Sterne's levity.[11] It was not until 1941 that B. H. Lehman observed that *Tristram Shandy* contained the "theme of procreation", the proper one for comedy.[12]

Sterne's having Tristram say that he "began his book by writing the first sentence and trusting to Almighty God for the second"[13] was taken seriously. On the other hand, another statement, made near the beginning, seems to have been regarded as inconsequential:

But I was begot and born to misfortunes; ... so that I was doom'd by marriage articles to have my nose squeezed as flat to my face, as if the destinies had actually spun me without one.
How this event came about, and what a train of vexatious disappointments, in one stage or other of my life, have pursued me

---

[9] *The Works of William Makepeace Thackeray*, DeLuxe ed. (New York, Bretano's, 1878-86), IX, p. 363.
[10] George Saintsbury in "Introduction", *The Life and Opinions of Tristram Shandy, Gentleman* (London, J. M. Dent & Sons, 1894), p. xxl.
[11] "Introduction", to *A Sentimental Journey Through France and Italy*, World's Classics ed. (London, Oxford University Press, 1948), p. xv.
[12] "Of Time, Personality, and the Author", *University of California Studies in English*, VII (1941), pp. 233-250. Thirteen years later he discussed the procreation theme with *Tristram Shandy* as one example of several wherein comedy was so informed: "Comedy and Laughter", *University of California Studies in English*, X (1954), pp. 81-104. See also suggestions for analyzing the structure of *Tristram Shandy* in terms of Lehman's theory in Dorothy Van Ghent, *The English Novel: Form and Function* (New York, Rinehart, 1953), pp. 85-98 and 336-346.
[13] James Aiken Work (ed.), *Tristram Shandy*, p. 540. Cited hereafter as *Tristram Shandy*.

from the mere loss, or rather compression, of this one single member, shall be laid before the reader in due time.¹⁴

What appears to be too serious a statement of purpose to be neglected was likewise ignored.¹⁵ At the end of the fourth volume and near enough the middle of the work to merit consideration as being a statement about a turning point or change, Sterne had Tristram say

> From this point I am to be considered as heir apparent to the Shandy family – and it is from this point properly that the story of my Life and Opinions sets out; with all my hurry and precipitation I have been clearing the ground to raise the building – and such a building do I foresee it will turn out, as never was planned, and as never was executed since Adam....
> The thing I lament is that things have crowded in so thick upon me, that I have not been able to get into that part of my work, towards which, I have all the way, looked forwards, with so much earnest desire; and that is the campaigns, but especially the amours of my uncle Toby....¹⁶

Likewise ignored was Yorick's answer to Elizabeth Shandy's query of what the story was all about. Not until a very few years ago was it considered that Sterne had concluded the book instead of "letting his pen drop".¹⁷

The work, it seems, was thought to be as devoid of purpose as of structure. If the author's declaration to Dodsley (the prospective printer of *Tristram Shandy*) was known, it appears to have been disregarded:

> The plan as you may perceive, is a most extensive one – taking in, not only the weak part of the sciences, in which the true point of ridicule lies – but everything else, which I have found laugh-at-able in my way.¹⁸

---

¹⁴ *Ibid.*, p. 39.
¹⁵ Ernest A. Baker, *History of the English Novel* (New York, Barnes & Noble, 1930), IV, p. 255, comments on the disparity between Sterne's announcement of purpose and his performance.
¹⁶ *Tristram Shandy*, p. 336.
¹⁷ Wayne C. Booth, "Did Sterne Complete *Tristram Shandy*?", *MP*, XLVIII (1951), pp. 172-183.
¹⁸ Lewis Perry Curtis (ed.), *Letters of Laurence Sterne* (Oxford, Clarendon Press, 1935), p. 74. Cited hereafter as *Letters*.

Statements of purpose within *Tristram Shandy* itself apparently went unnoticed. Little attention was given to Sterne's having said in the preface to volumes three and four that the "intent was to write a good book . . . a wise, aye and a discreet [one]".[19] For that matter, equally ignored was Yorick's final evaluation of the work as a story about "A COCK and a BULL . . . And one of the best of its kind I ever heard". It seems to have been regarded as a description of the chaotic nature of the book or the last of many bawdy jests in it.

Identification of Sterne and his work may have hindered not only recognition of the structure and purpose of *Tristram Shandy* but also perception of the complexity and depth of the characters in it. Uncle Toby, who was too sensitive of the common brotherhood of all creatures to hurt a fly, was seen as a projection of the man who had the same extra-sensitive feelings and "the shallow philosophy" that "could ignore the necessity for killing insects".[20] Sterne was believed to have the same feelings because he had made Uncle Toby. The subtlety of Sterne and the complexity of Uncle Toby went unnoticed. The critics of *Tristram Shandy* overlooked the fact that in several cases Sterne showed the callousness as well as the gentleness of Uncle Toby. Captain Shandy cut off the tops of the ancestral jack boots without caring how Walter felt about them. To carry on his war games, he borrowed a hundred pounds from his brother without any intention of repaying the loan. If LeFevre's dying had not prevented it, Uncle Toby would have added nursing to his crippled servant's duties. He was not only the cause of the window-sash accident, but also petulant enough to threaten to "spring a mine, blow up his fortifications", and kill everybody if Walter complained about Trim's removing the window weights. In spite of Uncle Toby's defections he and the author were regarded as being highly sensitive to the feelings of others.

A deviation from the traditional view occurred when Coleridge saw that Trim's funeral sermon for Bobby was "in contrast to a

---

[19] *Tristram Shandy*, pp. 192-193.
[20] Howes, pp. 54 f.

Jacobean context".[21] He attributed the callousness to Sterne however, for he did not consider that Sterne might have been presenting the context as Tristram's writing.

The identification of Sterne with Tristram can easily lead to untenable conclusions. Although Tristram's standing with his garters in his hand, lamenting that which would not pass, has not been offered as evidence that Sterne had suffered a near mutilation, a recent critic has rested part of his case for Sterne's having a veneral disease on Work's observation that "the suspicion of sexual impotence ... hangs like a dubious halo over the head of every Shandy male, including the bull".[22] It seems that if a better reason for the Shandean impotency beyond the fact of its being "laugh-at-able" is needed, it might be found by examining the way in which Walter Shandy's belief in the superiority of the male in procreation is successively discredited.[23]

The identification of the author and his work is as old as *Tristram Shandy*. When the last volume of the novel appeared in 1767, some of the members of Sterne's public urged the Archbishop of York to "deter this wanton Scandal to his cloth from proceeding in this Lewd Ludicrous manner as he has long done to the shame and disgrace of his Sacred Order and the detriment of Society".[24] Sterne, knowing that he was held responsible for Tristram Shandy's lack of decorum, faintly protested to an unidentified correspondent: "The world has imagined because I wrote 'Tristram Shandy' that I was more Shandean than I really was." [25]

It is difficult to ascertain whether or not Sterne felt any assurance that his works would long outlast himself. Even the prophecy that the book would "swim down the gutter of time with *The*

[21] Thomas M. Raysor (ed.), *Coleridge's Miscellaneous Criticism* (Cambridge, Harvard University Press, 1936), p. 126.
[22] A. R. Towers, "Sterne's Cock and Bull Story", *ELH*, XXIV (March, 1957), pp. 12-20. See also Work's comments in his "Introduction" to *Tristram Shandy*, p. lx.
[23] See below, pp. 24-25.
[24] *Letters*, p. 301, n. 2.
[25] *Ibid.*, pp. 402-403; Virginia Woolf in "Introduction", *A Sentimental Journey*, p. xiii, says that the remark was made by Sterne to Lord Shelburne.

Legation of Moses and *A Tale of A Tub*"²⁶ was made by Tristram instead of Sterne. And it is at least equally uncertain that Sterne was aware of the harm identification might do to himself and his work. At any rate, he seems to have done little to direct the stream of criticism at the beginning.²⁷

Three of his contemporaries, one of whom thought *Tristram Shandy* would not last, were far more instrumental than the author in directing the stream of criticism at the beginning. They were Johnson, Boswell, and Walpole.

Of the three, Walpole perhaps did Sterne the most harm by making the following statement:

What is called sentimental writing, though it be understood to appeal solely to the heart, may be the product of a bad one. One would imagine that Sterne had been a man of a very tender heart – yet I know from indubitable authority, that his mother, who kept a school, having run in debt, on account of an extravagant daughter, would have rotted in jail, if the parents of her scholars had not raised a subscription for her. Her son had too much sentiment to have any feeling. A dead ass was more important to him than a living mother.²⁸

The last sentence was particularly harmful when it was popularized in the following century by Lord Byron.²⁹ Although twentieth-century research has fairly well refuted the charge against Sterne of permitting his mother to starve,³⁰ it has yet to drop the charge against him and indict Tristram Shandy for weeping over the dead ass.

Bowsell, of course, exercised less influence by what he said about Sterne and *Tristram Shandy* than by perpetuating what Samuel Johnson had said about them. It can be argued that Johnson's pronouncement, that the book had not lasted because it was

---

²⁶ *Tristram Shandy*, p. 610.
²⁷ Howes in *Yorick and the Critics*, p. 6, n. 7, comments that "the confusion was of Sterne's own making, and it has colored critical appraisals both of his own day and of posterity".
²⁸ *Ibid.*, pp. 89-90.
²⁹ Roland E. Prothero (ed.), *Works of Lord Byron, Prose* (London and New York, J. Murray and Scribner's, 1898-1904), II, p. 359. See below p. 22.

odd,[31] harmed neither author nor book. Even if the judgment was wrong, the book was judged by whatever merit Johnson believed it possessed. He again judged it by its own merits instead of by its author when he remarked that he read it on a stage journey, but he would not have done so had he been at large. For Johnson to have disliked *Tristram Shandy* is scarcely surprising; still, it can be wondered why he did not have a good word for its erudition. It also seems that since he greatly admired Burton's *Anatomy of Melancholy*, he would have been attracted by its like elements in Sterne's book. Johnson, of course, was not to become famous for lacking prejudices.

Johnson, nevertheless, appears to have kept separate his dislike for Sterne and his dislike for *Tristram Shandy*. He would naturally have been offended by unbecoming levity on the part of a priest; he would have been offended also by Sterne's wit in the sermons; [32] and he would have been irritated with *Tristram Shandy* for the reason he gave, its oddity.

At the beginning of the nineteenth century Dr. John Ferriar's *Illustrations of Sterne* presented fairly conclusive evidence of Sterne's extensive borrowing from Burton's *Anatomy of Melancholy*.[33] According to Ferriar, Sterne had also borrowed not only from Montaigne, Bacon, Blount, Bishop Hall, and Swift, but from Rabelais, Beroalde, D'Aubigne, Bruscambille, and Scarron. Ferriar maintained that Sterne revealed his character by the nature of his borrowing from Rabelais and the other writers in the last group:

Sterne's imagination, untamed by labour, and unsated by a long acquaintance with literary folly, dwelt with enthusiasm on the grotesque pictures of manners and opinions, displayed in his favorite authors.[34]

[31] James Boswell, *Life of Samuel Johnson, L.L.D.*, edited by George Birbeck Hill, revised and enlarged by Laurence F. Powell (Oxford, Clarendon Press, 1934, 1950), II, p. 449.
[32] Work repeats the comments of Johnson in "Introduction", *Tristram Shandy*, pp. xxxi and xxiv.
[33] *Illustrations of Sterne; with other Essays and Verses* (London, Printed in Manchester, 1798). A revised edition appeared in 1821 (2 vols.; London, Cadell and Davies).
[34] Quoted in Howes, *Yorick and the Critics*, p. 85, from the first edition

In the first half of the nineteenth century Sterne and his work continued to be identified. With the exception of Byron, the leading Romanticists appeared to have regarded Sterne in a more kindly fashion than some of his contemporaries had. Four of them – Coleridge, Hazlitt, Scott, and Carlyle – insisted on his greatness.

Although Coleridge observed "individual peculiarity" in some of the characters in *Tristram Shandy*,[35] he did not see it in Tristram, nor did he recognize Tristram Shandy as a delegated writer with a personality of his own. For Coleridge "the humour in *Tristram Shandy* was the humorist's own oddity".[36] And for Coleridge the humorist was Laurence Sterne. He nevertheless provided what may well prove to be the correct interpretation of Yorick's comment that *Tristram Shandy* was a cock-and-bull story: "Sterne made the great little and the little great in order to destroy both, because all is equal in contrast with the infinite." [37]

Hazlitt who contended that the great writers create characters "that speak like men, not authors",[38] praised Sterne for creating the characters of Yorick, Dr. Slop, Walter Shandy, Uncle Toby, Trim, Susannah, and the Widow Wadman.[39] But Hazlitt overlooked Tristram as a character in or the narrator of *Tristram Shandy*.

Sir Walter Scott, who failed to see the importance of the character Tristram, managed, nevertheless, to come close to seeing it: "For it is mainly in Walter Shandy's character that Sterne finds a convenient repository for the great quantity of extraordinary reading and antiquated learning he had collected." [40] Scott either failed to notice or to remark that Walter Shandy was not the sole repository. Uncle Toby had read several books; even the Widow Wadman had read three or four, Yorick was well read, and Tris-

---
of the *Illustrations*. The revised edition of the *Illustrations* repeats the statement on pp. 22-23 of Vol. II.
[35] Raysor (ed.), *Coleridge's Miscellaneous Criticism*, p. 123.
[36] *Ibid*.
[37] *Ibid.*, p. 119.
[38] P. P. Howes (ed.), *William Hazlitt: Complete Works*, "Centenary ed." (London and Toronto, J. M. Dent, 1930-1934), V, p. 185.
[39] *Ibid.*, VI, p. 121.
[40] Sir Walter Scott (ed.), *The Novels of Sterne, Goldsmith, Dr. Johnson, Mackenzie, Horace Walpole, and Clara Reeve*, "Ballantyne Series" (London, Printed in Edinburgh, 1923), "Introduction" to Vol. V.

tram had read theirs and Walter's books and many others besides. Since Scott's edition of *Tristram Shandy* (with his introduction) was for many years the form in which the work was chiefly available, his influence on Sterne's reputation was considerable.[41] If Scott had only been able to go one step further and see Tristram as the repository and the principal character, he might have rendered a more valuable service to man and book.

After capitalizing on the public's identifying him with his *Childe Harold* and *Don Juan*, Byron should have been aware of the disparity in his own case,[42] and have recognized the disparity in Sterne's. But instead of doing so, Byron repeated the remark of Walpole's in writing of himself: "Ah, I am as bad as that dog Sterne, who preferred whining over 'a dead ass to relieving a living mother' – villain – hypocrite – slave – sycophant! but I am no better." [43] There is some reason to believe that Byron had read Sterne's works. Elizabeth Boyd writes that "while Byron was re-reading Fielding in Italy, he did not neglect Sterne. He quotes occasionally from *A Sentimental Journey* in his letters, and the remnants of his library sold in 1827 contained a copy of *Tristram Shandy*". After citing two stanzas from *Don Juan*, Canto II, she remarks:

There is more than mere imitation of tone, vocabulary, and sentence structure here. Byron had put on, at least for the moment, the very garment of Sterne's humor – gallantry, sentiment, naughtiness, philosophy, and high comedy blended together.[44]

Byron's popularity has been credited with giving currency to the remarks about Sterne's filial cruelty and maudlin sentimentality.[45] It should also be credited with promoting the identification of Sterne and his putative authors.

[41] Howes, *Yorick and the Critics*, pp. 119-122.
[42] Louis I. Bredvold in "Introduction", to his edition of *Don Juan and Other Satirical Essays* (New York, Odyssey Press, 1935), p. v.
[43] Rowland E. Prothero (ed.), *Letters and Journals: Works of Lord Byron* (London, John Murray, 1922; New York, Charles Scribner's Sons, 1922), II, p. 350. According to Prothero, Byron made the entry in his *Journal* in 1813. The *Letters and Journals* were published in 1830.
[44] *Byron's Don Juan: A Critical Study* (New York, Humanities Press, 1958), pp. 56 f.
[45] Howes, *Yorick and the Critics*, p. 90, n. 4.

Another, although a later figure in the Romantic Period, Thomas Carlyle, not only called Sterne "our best, our finest, if not our strongest specimen of humour",[46] but also incorporated no little of *Tristram Shandy* in his *Sartor Resartus*.[47] In at least one instance he identified his source: "O my friends, we are (in Yorick Sterne's words) but as 'turkeys driven, with a stick and a red clout to market'." According to Charles F. Harrold, Carlyle's style owed something to Sterne.[48]

One student of Carlyle has found evidence that *Tristram Shandy* suggested the clothes philosophy in *Sartor Resartus*.[49] Although Carlyle owed much to Sterne and in many ways acknowledged his indebtedness, he nevertheless contributed to the identification of the man and his work. In his *Life of Frederick the Great* he identified Uncle Toby with Roger Sterne:

> Sputtering of War; that is to say, Siege of Gibraltar. A siege utterly unmemorable, and without the least interest for existing mankind with their ungrateful humour, – if it be not once more that the Father of *Tristram Shandy* was in it.... The poor Lieutenant Father died soldiering in the West Indies, soon after this; and we shall not mention him again. But History ought to remember that he is "Uncle Toby", and take her measures.[50]

For the Victorian Period Thackeray has been credited with causing Sterne's works to be considered bad because the man was bad. Virginia Woolf held the "arrogant Victorians" responsible for accepting his slanderous remark that " 'there is not a page of Sterne's writing but has something better away, a latent corrup-

---

[46] Thomas Carlyle, *Critical and Miscellaneous Essays* (ed.), H. B. Traill, "Centenary ed." (New York, Charles Scribner's Sons, 1904), I, p. 17.
[47] Charles F. Harrold in his edition of *Sartor Resartus* (New York, Odyssey Press, 1937), notes indebtedness to Sterne on pages 12, 14, 30, 62, 64, 66, 87, 105, 131, 148, and 170. Harrold also observes on p. 12, n. 3, that the subtitle of *Sartor Resartus, The Life and Opinions of Herr Teufelsdröckh*, was "probably suggested by Sterne's *The Life and Opinions of Tristram Shandy* ... one of Carlyle's early favorites".
[48] *Ibid.*, p. 63.
[49] Hill Shine, *Carlyle's Early Reading to 1834* (Lexington, University of Kentucky Libraries, 1953), p. 281, No. 281; on page 352 Shine records 28 allusions to Sterne in Carlyle's reading up to 1834.
[50] *History of Frederick the Great* (New York, Charles Scribner's Sons, 1903), II, pp. 98 f.

tion – a hint of an impure presence' ".[51] Howes recently has agreed with her, although he believes Thackeray's criticism was self-projection.[52]

Fitzgerald's *Life of Sterne* (1864), was the first full-length biography of Laurence Sterne.[53] Fitzgerald contended for a more lenient view of the man. Sterne, he argued, should be forgiven his indiscretions and commended for his hitherto unpublicized good actions. Although he held the old principle that as the man was so was the work, he still did the artist a service by insisting that Sterne had exercised care in revising *Tristram Shandy* for publication:

Mr. Sterne had actually recast this book, cut away all provincial allusions, made the satire general, notes are added when wanted, and the whole made more saleable, about 150 pages added; and to conclude, a strong interest formed and forming in its behalf.[54]

Walter Bagehot, who reviewed in the same article Fitzgerald's *Life* and a biography of Thackeray,[55] made some statements about Sterne and his work that the twentieth century can accept as relevant criticism. In the first place, he called Sterne "an old flirt".[56] Since an old flirt has to be gratified more by imagination than by reality, Sterne's *Letters to Eliza* [57] can be regarded as more foolish than scandalous. In the second place, Bagehot argued that because Sterne was a pagan at heart, he should not have entered the church.[58] That the tone of Sterne's sermons did not sound right to Bagehot is perhaps less important for us than that Sterne's

[51] Quoted in Virginia Woolf's "Introduction", *A Sentimental Journey*, p. xv.
[52] Howes, *Yorick and the Critics*, p. 146.
[53] Percy Fitzgerald, *Life of Laurence Sterne* (London, Chapman and Hall).
[54] *Ibid.*, I, pp. 361-362.
[55] Howes in *Yorick and the Critics*, p. 161, states that the article appeared in the *National Review* for April, 1864. Passages cited here are found in "Sterne and Thackeray", in *Literary Studies by Walter Bagehot*, "Introduction" by George Sampson (London and New York, J. M. Dent & E. P. Dutton, 1911), II, pp. 94-129.
[56] *Ibid.*, p. 118.
[57] Cf. Alice Green Fredman, *Diderot and Sterne* (New York, Columbia University Press, 1955), p. 43.
[58] Bagehot, "Sterne and Thackeray", p. 97.

paganism might reveal a new dimension in *Tristram Shandy* and in *A Sentimental Journey*.[59]

Bagehot also said some things about *Tristram Shandy* as a work of fiction. Although he objected to "fantastic disorder of the form",[60] he was enthusiastic in his praise of Sterne's delineation of "common human action".[61] The only fault contained "no half-commonplace personages" to bridge the gap between the "central group of singular person" and the world.[62] Evidently, he did not consider the possibility of Parson Yorick's being that half-commonplace personage. Despite his taking a side in the old argument over the offensiveness of the filth by reiterating that Sterne was "indecent for the sake of indecency",[63] his criticism was salutary. It directed some attention to *Tristram Shandy* as a work of fiction.

Bagehot's evaluation of Sterne and *Tristram Shandy* was apparently less influential on the latter part of the nineteenth century than were Thackeray's denunciations of Sterne, for Sterne continued to be regarded as the licentious and lachrymose man, who had written a dirty, chaotic book and a sentimental journal. Another biography of Sterne appeared before the century ended.[64] It, however, appeared to make less impression than Sir Sidney Lee's sketch of Sterne in the *Dictionary of National Biography*.[65]

It remained for the twentieth century to take a serious interest

---

[59] B. H. Lehman, "Comedy and Laughter", *In Five Gayley Lectures* (Berkeley and Los Angeles, University of California Press, 1954), p. 85. See also Rufus D. Putney, "Laurence Sterne, Apostle of Laughter", in *The Age of Johnson: Essays Presented to Chauncey Brewster Tinker* (New Haven, Yale University Press, 1949), p. 170. Putney has concluded that "Sterne's clerical vocation gave him the absolute ethical code that made possible the dispassionate judgment comedy requires. ... By making him take thought it added to his greatness as a writer."
[60] Bagehot, p. 105.
[61] *Ibid.*, p. 104.
[62] *Ibid.*, p. 110.
[63] *Ibid.*, p. 108.
[64] H. D. Traill, *Sterne*, "English Men of Letters" (London, MacMillan, 1911).
[65] Vols. pp. 52-54 (Shearman-Stovin) were published 1897-1898 under the editorship of Sir Sidney Lee. See published note to Vol. I (Oxford, Oxford University Press, 1921-1922).

in Sterne and his works. So prolific has been the Sterne scholarship and criticism that only the more important editors, biographers, and critics can be mentioned.

Wilbur L. Cross edited the *Works* in 1904 [66] and in 1908 published his *Life and Times of Laurence Sterne*.[67] Lewis Melville shortly afterwards published *The Life and Letters of Laurence Sterne*,[68] breaking ground for Lewis Perry Curtis' definitive edition of the *Letters*, that was to appear a quarter of a century later.[69] In 1913 C. E. Vaughan in the *Cambridge History of English Literature* recognized Sterne as the eighteenth-century writer responsible for giving greater freedom to the novel.[70] In 1928 Sir Herbert Read in *English Prose Style* included him among his half-dozen greatest writers of English prose.[71] The following year Read concluded in the *Sense of Glory* that Sterne's heroes transcended those of the Renaissance, because they are "at once mythical and human, and therefore held by us in a relation of both grandeur and intimacy".[72] The year 1929 witnessed the publication of two important works on Sterne: the definitive edition of the *Life* by Wilbur L. Cross [73] and the World's Classics edition of *A Sentimental Journey*, with an introduction by Virginia Woolf.[74]

The thirties began with Ernest A. Baker's devoting to Sterne several pages of harsh criticism in the *History of the English*

---

[66] Wilbur L. Cross, *The Works and Life of Laurence Sterne*, 12 Vols. (New York, J. F. Taylor, 1904).
[67] Wilbur L. Cross, *The Works and Life of Laurence Sterne* (New York, MacMillan Co., 1908).
[68] Lewis Melville [Lewis Saul Benjamin], *The Life and Letters of Laurence Sterne* (London, S. Paul and Co., 1911).
[69] Lewis Perry Curtis (ed.), *Letters of Laurence Sterne* (Oxford, Clarendon Press, 1935).
[70] "Sterne and the Novel of His Times", in *Cambridge History of English Literature*, X, pp. 44-66.
[71] Herbert Read, *English Prose Style* (New York, Henry Holt and Co., 1928), p. xiii.
[72] Herbert Read, "Sterne", in *Sense of Glory* (New York, Harcourt, Brace & Co., 1930), p. 151; (Cambridge, Cambridge University Press, 1929), p. 252.
[73] Wilbur L. Cross, *The Life and Times of Laurence Sterne*, 3d. ed. rev. (New Haven, Yale University Press, 1929).
[74] See above, p. 15.

THE AUTHOR AND HIS WORK 27

Novel [75] and with Charles Whibley's making more easily available for scholars the catalogue of Sterne's library, sold at auction a few months after Sterne's death.[76] Lewis Perry Curtis, who in 1929 had examined the politics of Sterne [77] and in 1930 had determined that Ann Ward was the first printer of *Tristram Shandy*,[78] in 1935 published the definitive edition of Sterne's letters. The next year, 1936, was fruitful for Sterne criticism. Thomas M. Raysor's edition of *Coleridge's Miscellaneous Criticism* made Coleridge's evaluation of Sterne more readily available than it had been.[79] Theodore Baird demonstrated that Sterne had used time in *Tristram Shandy* in a responsible fashion.[80] And Kenneth MacLean argued convincingly that Sterne had used John Locke's association of ideas as a unifying principle in *Tristram Shandy*.[81] Watkins insisted on the serious purpose of Sterne in writing "against the spleen" in order to make his troubles bearable.[82]

The forties began with James Aiken Work's edition of *Tristram Shandy* for the Odyssey Press. It was "a reprint of the first London edition of each of the nine volumes of the work – the latest edition which Sterne himself saw through the press".[83] It was also annotated "to place at the disposal of the modern reader some of the information which Sterne assumed his intelligent contemporaries to possess".[84] Work, furthermore, wrote an introduction, consonant in critical acuity with his editorial achieve-

[75] Ernest A. Baker, *The History of the English Novel*, 10 Vols. (New York, Barnes and Noble, 1930), IV, pp. 240-276.
[76] *A Facsimile Reproduction of a Unique Catalogue of Laurence Sterne's Library*, Introduction by Charles Whibley (London, Tregaskis; New York, Wells, 1930).
[77] *The Politics of Laurence Sterne* (Oxford, Oxford University Press).
[78] "The First Printer of *Tristram Shandy*", *PMLA*, XLVII (1930), pp. 777-789.
[79] See above, pp. 11 f.
[80] "The Time Scheme of *Tristram Shandy*", *PMLA*, II (1936), pp. 803-820.
[81] *John Locke and English Literature of the Eighteenth Century* (New Haven, Yale University Press), "Preface", *passim*, and particularly pp. 86 and 132.
[82] "Yorick Revisited", in *Perilous Balance: The Tragic Genius of Johnson, Swift, and Sterne* (Princeton, Princeton University Press), pp. 99-157.
[83] *Tristram Shandy*, p. lxxv.
[84] *Ibid.*, pp. lx-lxxv.

ment. In the following year B. H. Lehman presented his highly important analysis of the purpose of *Tristram Shandy*,[85] which was to be followed thirteen years later by his demonstration that procreation is the proper theme for comedy.[86] Sterne's sermons [87] were finally subjected to the like kind of scholarly study the letters had received in the thirties. Before the forties were out, George Sherburn in *A Literary History of England* designated Sterne as the most eminent novelist in the period from 1760 to 1800.[88]

The fifties continued to enlarge the interpretation of Sterne's works. In 1948 Ernest Dilworth had argued that the present-day meaning of "sentimental" would not hold good for Sterne or for his writing.[89] In 1951 D. W. Jefferson denied the oddity of *Tristram Shandy* by placing Sterne among the learned wits who followed the tradition established by Rabelais. Within the tradition Sterne "asserted his immortality most vigorously".[90] Wayne Booth in the following year demonstrated that Sterne's self-conscious mode of narration was also traditional.[91] John Traugott in 1954 attacked another long-held opinion concerning Sterne. He argued that Sterne, instead of being a disciple of John Locke, used *Tristram Shandy* to demonstrate the fallaciousness of the Lockean system.[92] In 1951 Wayne Booth, by marshalling evidence that Sterne completed *Tristram Shandy*, had attacked still another

---

[85] "Of Time, Personality and the Author", *University of California Studies in English*, VII (1941), pp. 233-250.

[86] "Comedy and Laughter", *University of California Studies in English*, X (1954), pp. 81-101.

[87] Lansing Van der Hammond, *Laurence Sterne's Sermons of Mr. Yorick* (New Haven, Yale University Press, 1948).

[88] Albert C. Baugh and Others (eds.), *A Literary History of England* (New York, Appleton-Century-Crofts, 1948), p. 1042.

[89] *The Unsentimental Journey of Laurence Sterne* (New York, The King's Crown Press, 1948).

[90] D. W. Jefferson, "*Tristram Shandy* and the Tradition of Learned Wit", *Essays in Criticism*, I (1951), pp. 225-248. Quotation is from T. S. Eliot, "Tradition and the Individual Talent", in *Selected Essays 1917-1932* (New York, Harcourt Brace & Co., 1932), p. 4.

[91] "The Self-Conscious Narrator in Comic Fiction before *Tristram Shandy*", *PMLA*, LXVII (1952), pp. 163-185.

[92] *Tristram Shandy's World: Sterne's Philosophical Rhetoric* (Berkeley and Los Angeles, University of California Press).

of the long-held opinions.[93] Three recent works on Sterne are Fredman's comparison of Sterne and Diderot,[94] Willard Connely's study of Sterne's life after 1760,[95] and R. B. M. Shaw's *The Making of a Humorist*.[96] Finally, the body of Sterne criticism has begun to be assesed with Howe's *Yorick and the Critics*.[97] One of the most useful aids for studying the structure of *Tristram Shandy* has appeared in Dorothy Van Ghent's textbook for studying the novel.[98]

Despite the wealth of recent scholarship and criticism, the relation of Sterne to his work is still subject to confusion. On the one hand, although much has been done that reveals the excellence of *Tristram Shandy*, there is the danger of crediting it with more structural qualities than it possesses and of losing sight of Laurence Sterne. To do so is to neglect the conditions in Sterne's life, prior to his writing, which affected the way he began writing it and those after he began writing which determined the course his novel took.

On the other hand, the biographical criticism which equates Sterne and Tristram still exerts its influence. Wilbur Cross, admirable though his work remains, is perhaps the chief offender. That Sterne's life could in part be reconstructed from Sterne's works was no more than Cross's opinion; but since Cross relied upon it in writing the biography, it became something more than opinion and perpetuated the damaging identification:

And if the reader discovers, as he will, that *Tristram Shandy* and the *Sentimental Journey* are in part autobiography, and that their author was as strange a compound of whims as they, then new points of vantage may be gained for viewing and judging Sterne stage by stage

---

[93] "Did Sterne Complete Tristram Shandy?", *MP*, XLVIII (1951), pp. 172-183.
[94] Alice Green Fredman, *Diderot and Sterne* (New York, Columbia University Press, 1955).
[95] *Laurence Sterne as Yorick* (London, Bodley Head, 1958).
[96] *Laurence Sterne: The Making of a Humorist, 1713-1762* (London, Richards Press, 1957).
[97] Alan B. Howes, *Yorick and the Critics: Sterne's Reputation in England, 1760-1868* (New Haven, Yale University Press, 1958).
[98] *The English Novel: Form and Function* (New York, Rinehart, 1953), pp. 85-98 and 336-346.

in his career, and for achieving a final portrait of the man in relation to his work.[99]

Although it is difficult to gainsay the value of James Aiken Work's "Introduction" to the edition of *Tristram Shandy*, it is, nevertheless, evident that Work carried on Cross's identification of Sterne and his writing:

> As Sterne was also a humorist – "the most complete example in modern literature", Cross has called him, "of a man whose other faculties are overpowered by a sence of humor" – so *Tristram Shandy* is above all else a humorous book.[100]

Lewis Perry Curtis has left little doubt about what his opinion of Sterne and his writing was:

> With little ability to conceive a character apart from himself, he unconsciously watched his own reflection and supposed it to be variously Walter or Tristram Shandy or Parson Yorick or even Uncle Toby.[101]

And finally, there was Virginia Woolf, who knew Sterne's writing well, and whose own writing probably was influenced by it.[102] Her opinion about the relation of the man and his work has not been taken lightly. Her remarks almost justify Walter Shandy's statement that "words have a magic bias of their own". Virginia Woolf looked upon the *Sentimental Journey* as Sterne's own journey, and the reader could scarcely assume that she set *Tristram Shandy* apart from the author's other works:

> Nobody, of course, stood more in need of liberty to be himself than Sterne. For while there are writers whose gift is impersonal, so that a Tolstoy, for example, can create a character which has no shred of his personality attached to it, Sterne's always included a large part of himself. Little or nothing of *A Sentimental Journey* would be left if all that we call Sterne were extracted from it.[103]

---

[99] *Life*, 3d. ed. rev. (1929), p. xiii.
[100] Cross (ed.), *Tristram Shandy*, p. li.
[101] *Letters*, p. xxx.
[102] E. M. Forster, *Aspects of the Novel* (New York, Harcourt Brace & Co., 1927), pp. 34-38. See also Melvin Friedman, *Stream of Consciousness: A Study in Literary Method* (New Haven, Yale University Press, 1955), p. 28: For opposing view see Miriam Allot, *Novelists on the Novel* (London, Routledge and Kegan Paul, 1959), p. 168.
[103] World's Classics edition, p. viii.

THE AUTHOR AND HIS WORK

Two instances may be cited as evidence that the confusion is still being made. As recently as 1958 a biographer of Sterne, one who has had advantage of the Sterne criticism and scholarship of the last twenty years, still insisted on the identification. He used for an epigraph a quotation from Dominique-Joseph Garat (1745-1835): "Never was an author more like his works; to read them, or to see and hear him was almost the same thing." [104] Only four years earlier, a critic of Sterne had stated as a fact the conclusion implied by those who insisted on the identification:

> For he was not a "novelist". A critic looking at Sterne as a chapter in the history of the novel will find him a sad case of arrested development.[105]

It seems reasonable to conclude that the relation of Sterne to his work has not yet been sufficiently established. One may assume that such is the case and hope that a modest effort will serve in part to establish it. The life and ministry of Laurence Sterne, therefore, will be re-examined for sources of the elements which were brought to artistic development in *Tristram Shandy*, and the novel itself will be re-examined for evidence of the author's *modus operandi*. Finally, a conclusion will be attempted in regard to the effect of the literary achievement upon the life of Laurence Sterne. In short, an attempt will be made to ascertain the relation of Sterne to *Tristram Shandy* and of *Tristram Shandy* to Sterne.

---

[104] Willard Connelly, *Laurence Sterne as Novelist*.
[105] Traugott, *Tristam Shandy's World*, p. 105.

II

THE MAN AND THE NOVELIST

In this chapter Sterne's life will be studied and compared with Tristram's, and phases of the author's life will be examined for their probable effect on the writing. The question of Yorick's identity and that of the influence of Sterne's ministry on the novel will be treated in a separate chapter.

For *Tristram Shandy* to be autobiographical, strict correspondence of the details in the life of Tristram with those in the life of Sterne is perhaps not a requisite; but, on the other hand, a disparity between the lives of Tristram Shandy and Laurence Sterne should affect the case for autobiography.

First of all, Sterne gave Tristram a different birth date from his own: "On the fifth day of November, 1718, . . . was I, Tristram Shandy, Gentleman, brought forth into this scurvy and disasterous [sic] world of ours." [1] In the "Memoirs" Sterne wrote of his own birth:

... I was born November 24th, 1713, a few days after my poor mother arrived from Dunkirk. – My birth-day was ominous to my poor father, who was, the day after our arrival with many other brave officers broke, and sent adrift into the wide world with a wife and two children.[2]

Although misfortune attended the births of Tristram and Sterne, and although both were born in November, there was a difference of nineteen days and almost five years. Such a slight difference in time, however, could be no more than a thin disguise for biography.

[1] *Tristram Shandy*, pp. 9 f.
[2] *Letters and Memoirs,* Vol. V: *Works of Laurence Sterne,* 7 Vols., Shakespeare Head ed. (Oxford, Blackwell, 1926-1927), p. 1.

But the dissimilarity of Tristram's and Sterne's relatives cannot be easily reconciled. Tristram's mother, for example, bears little resemblance to Sterne's. In the novel Sterne has had Tristram to present Elizabeth Shandy as a patient Griselda whose docility is a source of vexation to her husband, Walter Shandy. One of the best samples of her maddening acquiescence is in the "Bed of Justice" scene, where Walter tries to provoke her into disagreeing with him about the breeching of Tristram:

Order it as you please, Mr. *Shandy*, replied my mother, – But don't you think it right? added my father pressing the point to her. Perfectly, said my mother, if it pleases you, Mr. Shandy. There's for you, cried my father, losing his temper – Pleases me! . . .[3]

The author's mother, Agnes Sterne, was less agreeable. In his letter to his uncle, Jacques Sterne, Laurence Sterne described her as one who had dealt "barbarously" with him and had "grossly" deceived his uncle "by the misrepresentation" of his own "behavior to her".[4] Cross says of her that "she was no doubt vulgar, turbulent, and untrustworthy", and he adds, "Dr. Sterne himself, when he had no motive to the contrary, spoke of her temper as 'clamorous and rapacious!' "[5] What her disposition actually was is not so important, however, as what her son, the author of *Tristram Shandy*, thought it to be.

How little Tristram's father resembles Laurence Sterne's may be seen in the following passages.

Early in *Tristram Shandy* Sterne had Tristram describe Walter:

My father, you must know, who was originally a Turkey merchant, but had left off business for some years, in order to retire to, and die upon, his paternal estate in the county of ———, was I believe, one of the most regular men in everything he did, whether 'twas matter of business, or matter of amusement, that ever lived. . . . And being somewhere between fifty and sixty years of age, at the time I have been speaking of. . . .[6]

[3] *Tristram Shandy*, p. 438.
[4] Lewis Perry Curtis (ed.), *Letters of Laurence Sterne* (Oxford, Clarendon Press, 1935), p. 43.
[5] *Life*, p. 110.
[6] *Tristram Shandy*, p. 8.

In his "Memoirs", "set down for Lydia, in case she might have a curiosity, or a kinder motive to know them",[7] Sterne described his own father:

> Roger Sterne (grandson to Archbishop Sterne) Lieutenant in Handaside's regiment, was married to Agnes Hebert, widow of a captain of a good familiy ... her father-in-law [sic] was a noted sutler in Flanders, in Queen Ann's wars, where my father married his wife's daughter (N.B. he was in debt to him)....
>
> . . . .
>
> My father was a little smart man — active to the last degree, in all exercises — most patient of fatigues and disappointments, of which it pleased God to give him full measure — he was, in his temper somewhat rapid, and hasty — but of a kindly, sweet disposition, void of all design; and so innocent in his own intentions, that he suspected no one; so that you might have cheated him ten times in one day if nine had not been sufficient for your purpose....[8]

By further reading *Tristram Shandy*, one can find that a perverse fortune defeats Walter's plans for the geniture, name, and well-shaped nose of his son.

Objective biography has as yet revealed too little concerning Laurence Sterne's uncles to justify the identification of Uncle Toby with either of them. What is known about Richard Sterne's personality appears too meager for one to say that the man was like Captain Shandy.[9] And from the considerable amount known about Jacques Sterne, we know that the selfish, conniving churchman was entirely different from Uncle Toby.[10]

Carlyle's assumption that Uncle Toby was Roger Sterne does not have very much supporting evidence.[11] Both were, indeed, wounded soldiers; but they had been wounded differently. Uncle Toby had been wounded by a "blow from a stone, broke off from a parapet of a horn-work at the siege of Namur" (1695), "which struck full upon my uncle Toby's groin".[12] Roger Sterne, thirty-six years later (1731), "was run through the body by Captain

[7] *Works of Sterne*, V, p. 7.
[8] *Ibid.*, V, pp. 1, 4-5.
[9] *Life*, p. 26.
[10] *Ibid.*, pp. 71-72.
[11] See above, p. 23.
[12] *Tristram Shandy*, p. 67.

Phillips, in a duel (the quarrel began about a goose!)".[13] Uncle Toby's bout with the flux at the siege of Limerick (1690), was cured by an extravagant use of brandy.[14] On the other hand, Roger Sterne's attack of Jamaica fever in 1731 was fatal. Wrote Laurence Sterne in the "Memoirs":

He was sent to Jamaica, where he soon fell by the country fever, which took away his senses first, and made a child of him; and then, in a month or two walking about continually without complaining, till the moment he sat down in an armchair, and breathed his last.[15]

There is not only a discrepancy between the times when they were wounded and sickened but also a considerable difference between their ages. Roger Sterne died before he was forty; Uncle Toby is considerably older than forty at the time he is presented in *Tristram Shandy*; that is, in 1718, when Tristram was born.[16]

There are other differences between them. Uncle Toby Shandy apparently was impotent; Roger Sterne was the father of a family. Uncle Toby had long since retired from military service;[17] Roger died in service. A longer list might be made of their differences, but what their likenesses were, apparently, is a matter of conjecture.

It is also difficult to identify Walter Shandy with Laurence Sterne, although Sir Walter Scott believed that Walter had been made the repository of the author's vast store of erudition.[18]

There are several differences between Laurence Sterne and Walter Shandy: The one is a minister and the other is a retired merchant; the one a Cambridge graduate and the other a self-taught man (Tristram described Walter as θεοδίδακτος or taught of God);[19] the one a novelist and the other a man incapable of carrying out a writing project; the one an "old flirt" and the other a despiser of women; the one a legitimate member of the Sterne family and the other a man whose coat of arms bore the

[13] *Works of Sterne*, V, p. 4.
[14] *Tristram Shandy*, p. 401.
[15] *Works*, V, p. 4.
[16] *Tristram Shandy*, p. 9.
[17] *Ibid.*, pp. 78-79.
[18] See above, p. 21.
[19] *Tristram Shandy*, p. 52.

bend sinister.[20] And last of all, Laurence Sterne had no brother to correspond to Walter's.

But the chief identification has been that of Tristram with Laurence Sterne. And it is one that has come about despite certain important disparities. Sterne was a minister; Tristram Shandy's title of gentleman apparently means that Tristram was "a socially respectable person who had no specific occupation or profession".[21] Walter Shandy takes care to have his son properly educated and sent abroad; Roger Sterne depended upon his brothers, Richard and Jacques, to furnish his son with public school and Cambridge training.[22] Tristram is unmarried, apparently because of the window accident;[23] Laurence Sterne was married and was the father of two children.[24]

Tristram Shandy has been regarded as autobiographical, however, on grounds other than the coincidence of characters in the novel with people in real life. For one, it has been called "autobiographical" because it has been believed that Tristram's avowals of acting on impulse reveal Sterne's own lack of self-control. The kind of criticism is fairly recent that sees Tristram as Alan Dugald McKillop sees him.

He remains after all in command of the situations in which the other characters and the readers find themselves, in spite of the fact that he professes to be a victim of impulse, to be so busy that he doesn't know how he is going to get from one chapter to another.[25]

Furthermore, a brief review of the early years of Sterne's life, education, and reading does not bear out the old tradition that Sterne had been conditioned to be at the mercy of impulse.

Cross has reconstructed the first ten years of Sterne's childhood from the "Memoirs" and from *Tristram Shandy*:

Hard as were the many long journeys and migrations upon the young ensign and his wife during the subsequent years, the period must have been most agreeable to the boy himself. There were for him, who knew

[20] *Ibid.*, p. 20.
[21] *O.E.D.*, IV, p. 119. *Gentlemen*, 4.c.
[22] *Life*, pp. 17, 26.
[23] *Tristram Shandy*, p. 518.
[24] *Life*, pp. 61 f.
[25] *The Early Masters of English Fiction* (Lawrence, Kansas, The University of Kansas Press, 1956), p. 192.

nothing of the tragedy of it, pleasant sojourns in Wales and in the Isle of Wight, and a whole year in an Irish castle with relatives and friends....

He must have enjoyed, too, the large freedom of barrack life in England and in Ireland, however much it may have tested the endurance of his mother. There he met with new adventures and strange characters, the memory of which never left him. In after years, as he sat down in his Yorkshire parsonage to write his book, his childhood all came back to him – what he had seen with his own eyes and what his father had told him about the first serious engagement of the Thirty-Fourth Regiment of Foot in the battle of Wynendale, which Count de la Motte would have won, "had he not pressed on too speedily into the woods," and about the Treaty of Utrecht which broke my Uncle Toby's heart as well as sent Roger Sterne adrift into the world. Out of these memories, fortified by much reading of Marlborough's campaigns and enriched by later observations, came my uncle Toby, Trim, and Le Fever. Of no one more than of Sterne is the saying of Wordsworth truer that the child is father of the man.[26]

A recent biographer of Sterne has reconstructed a less pleasant picture of his childhood in the light of his mother's character:

After taking into account that her son's report of her unmotherly behavior was written in anger [the letter to Jacques Sterne], there remains enough for us to assume that she would hardly at any time have been a source of happiness and peace to her family. The home where she was wife and mother would have been the scene of many quarrels between herself and her kindly but hasty-tempered husband, and no place, therefore, in which a child could feel secure, or begin to develop a balanced personality.[27]

What effect the "tempering discipline" of the grammar school Laurence Sterne attended had on him is less conjectural.[28] For

[26] *Life*, pp. 16-17.
[27] Margaret R. B. Shaw, *The Making of a Humorist, 1713-1762* (London, Richards Press, 1957), pp. 4-5.
[28] J. W. Adamson, "Education", *From Steele and Addison to Pope and Swift*, Vol. IX: *Cambridge History of English Literature* (eds.), A. W. Ward and A. R. Waller (New York, G. P. Putnam's Sons, 1913; Cambridge, Cambridge University Press, 1913), pp. 425-462. See also Nicholas Sachs, *New Trends in Education in the Eighteenth Century* (London, Routledge and Kegan Paul, Ltd., 1951), pp. 37-62. See also Edward P. Cubberly, *History of Education* (New York, MacMillan Co., 1920), p. 438, and Paul Munroe, *A Text-Book of the History of Education* (New York, MacMillan Co., 1938), p. 524.

many years it was believed that Sterne escaped rigorous discipline by attending Heath Grammar School, the same school that Laurence's uncle, Richard Sterne, complained about to the Archbishop of York. But Cross, after weighing the claims of Heath and Hipporholme Grammar Schools, has concluded that Sterne attended Hipporholme. No evidence has been found concerning its inefficiency.[29]

Sterne's account, written nearly forty years afterwards,[30] of the ceiling-writing episode can be seen as some indication of the strictness of the school he attended.

My poor father died in March 1731. I remained at Halifax till about the latter end of that year, and cannot omit mentioning the episode of myself and the schoolmaster. – He had the ceiling of the room new-whitewashed; the ladder remained there; I one unlucky day mounted it, and wrote with a brush in large *capital* letters LAU. STERNE, for which the usher whipped me severely. My master was very much hurt at this, and said before me that never should that name be effaced, for I was a boy of genius, and he was sure I should come to preferment –. This expression made me forget the stripes I had received.[31]

It appears that the usher acted in accordance with the prevailing policy of the school, because Sterne felt the master's action had been extraordinary. Sterne asserted that "the expression made" him "forget the stripes", but he remembered them well enough to write about them forty years later.

In the second place, the school apparently required Sterne to apply himself to learning what it had to offer instead of permitting him to follow what his own whims might have dictated. Cross has argued that Sterne made good use of the time spent in public school:

Sterne there laid the foundation of a ready knowledge of the classical literatures. He learned to read and write Latin with great facility. Nearly all the authors in the usual curriculum of the period, he at some time quoted or referred to, evidently from memory. Horace came into his books perhaps more often than the rest. But Cicero, Pliny, Hesiod, and Isocrates are there also.[32]

[29] *Life*, p. 23.
[30] Shaw, *Making of a Humorist*, p. 5.
[31] *Sterne's Works*, V, p. 5.
[32] *Life*, p. 24.

Sterne was enabled to attend Cambridge by the aid of his cousin of Elvington and by that of a scholarship, endowed by his great-grandfather, the Archbishop of York. Although personal considerations probably were primarily responsible for his being given the scholarship and for his being helped by his cousin, the probability of Sterne's having given some indication of merit cannot be dismissed.

Possibly the lackadaisical nature of Sterne's years at Cambridge has been more emphasized than substantiated. Perhaps too much importance has been attached to the story of his tutor's wisely permitting him to follow his own bent and of his sprawling under a tree with John Hall-Stevenson reading whatever struck his fancy. Lodwick Hartley, for example, fancies that Sterne's years at Cambridge contributed little to mental discipline:

We can depend upon Laurie's not having taken too much interest in his studies; that is, insofar as the formalities were concerned. He could not have been a joy to his tutors. He disliked anything that required mental exertion and shared with Gray a thorough dislike for Cantabrigian metaphysics and mathematics. Naturally, logic and rhetoric under the guidance of a dry-as-dust don were dull and repulsive if they kept him from sprawling with Hall-Stevenson under the favorite walnut tree in the court of Jesus College, a volume of Rabelais in hand. And nothing that a tutor could offer or the college library supply could be so exciting as the poems of the scandalous Lord Rochester or a novel by the equally scandalous Aphra Behn.[33]

Peter Quennell also has made Sterne's residence at Cambridge sound carefree by alluding to the tutor, the playfellow, and the tree:

His tutor, ... let him have his way and, recognizing Sterne's singularity ... "did not trouble him with trammels." Among his contemporaries, he acquired a close and constant friend in John Hall, ... a languid and leisured dandy with whom he read Rabelais under the shade of an ancient walnut, called the Tree of Knowledge.[34]

[33] *This is Lorence: A Narrative of the Reverend Laurence Sterne* (Chapel Hill, The University of North Carolina Press, 1943), p. 18.
[34] *Four Portraits* (London, William Collins, 1945), in the U.S.: *The Profane Virtues* (Viking Press, 1945), p. 136. See also Willard Conneley, *Laurence Sterne as Yorick* (London, The Bodley Head, 1958), p. 21.

Cross's statement concerning the tradition, and his conclusions concerning the way Sterne spent his time at Cambridge present a different picture from that of Hartley and Quennell:

> Sterne's association with Hall-Stevenson would seem to be ample warrant for the tradition that he "was careless and inattentive to his book," that is, to the prescribed studies; that "he laughed a great deal, and sometime took the diversion of puzzling his tutors." But such a summary in a phrase or two is inexact and incomplete.[35]

Margaret R. B. Shaw denies that Sterne wasted his time:

> No doubt, in company with John Hall and other college jesters, he on occasion indulged in folly for folly's sake, eager to raise a laugh, and reckless of what means he took to do it. All the same, it was no mere buffoon who entered in 1733 on the books of so wise a college (as John Hall called it) nor in spite of a report that he "was careless and inattentive to his book", was it a student whose attention to the text could with any justice could be called perfunctory. Certainly we can believe that "he had a way of puzzling his tutors" by the little respect he showed for some of the works on the curriculum – but that is a different matter.[36]

Shaw believes, furthermore, that Sterne, while at Cambridge, followed a course of study that would have demanded effort.

> By the time Sterne left Cambridge he was well versed in Greek and Latin Literature ... and since he was preparing to enter the church, Sterne would not only have followed the usual course of undergraduate studies, but would also have read the works of eminent theologians and divines.[37]

On the basis of "the reading prescribed and recommended at Cambridge in Sterne's time" [38] and on the evidence he found in *Tristram Shandy*, Cross has concluded that Sterne "had read the books he was expected to know; and they were tucked away in his memory ready for his purposes when needed".[39] Although Cross

---

[35] *Life*, p. 28.
[36] *The Making of a Humorist*, pp. 21-22.
[37] *Ibid.*, p. 22. See also Nicholas Hans, *op. cit.*, p. 43, who observes that "life for servitors or Sizars [Sterne was one] was very hard ..., so farcical as for the wealthy student". Hans, furthermore, p. 51, offers evidence that the curriculum at Cambridge was "undoubtedly a full-time University curriculum".
[38] *Life*, p. 33, note.
[39] *Ibid.*, p. 34.

admits that Sterne had read Rabelais, Aphra Behn, Rochester, Wycherley, and Congreve, he insists that Sterne had also read several books of a more serious nature: Homer, Virgil, Theocritus, Pindar, Herodotus, Thucydides, Livy, and Tacitus. And Cross adds to the list Longinus, *On the Sublime*; Horace, *Ars Poetica*; Aristotle, *The Poetics*; Hobbes, *The Leviathan*; Burgerdicius, a Latin manual on logic; Puffendorf, an "immense work" entitled *The Law of Nature*; Cluver, *Germania Antiqua*; Newton, *Principia Mathematica*; and, of course, Locke, *Essay Concerning Human Understanding*.[40] Shaw adds to the list of Sterne's Cambridge reading the writings of Erasmus, Montaigne, Penelon, Le Bossu, the Church Fathers, and the Cambridge Platonists.[41] John Traugott, furthermore, argues that while at Cambridge Sterne had read closely Pierre Ramus' system of logic.[42]

Emphasis given to Sterne's dislike for the instruction at Cambridge and its use of formal logic has tended to obscure Sterne's having Tristram be something of a schoolman. Evidently, the four years in which Sterne encountered formal logic in reading, in the lecture halls, and in arguing set theses enabled him to create a Tristram who, unlike Walter, knew more than the names of the tools of logic.

When my father took me to Jesus College to enroll, ... it was a matter of just wonder to my worthy tutor, and two or three of the learned society, – that a man who knew not so much as the names of his tools, should be able to work after that fashion with them.[43]

Traugott has, in fact, found enough evidence in *Tristram Shandy* to sustain his thesis that Sterne wrote the book to contradict Locke's *Essay Concerning Human Understanding*.[44] But whether Sterne agreed with Locke or sought to contradict him, the mind of the creative artist appears to have been subjected to the discipline of the schoolmen.

[40] *Ibid.*, pp. 29-34.
[41] *The Making of a Humorist*, pp. 21-34.
[42] *Tristram Shandy's World* (Berkeley and Los Angeles, University of California Press, 1954), p. 66.
[43] *Tristram Shandy*, pp. 52-53.
[44] John Traugott, *Tristram Shandy's World* (Berkeley and Los Angeles, University of California Press, 1954).

One might suppose that if Sterne had lacked the years at Cambridge he might have written the kind of novel he has been credited with having produced, one with very little form or purpose. One can be more sure that Tristram and Walter Shandy are what they are because of the author's Cambridge training. It is interesting to notice that a group of Cambridge undergraduates, in February, 1760, passed a resolution to show its approval of *Tristram Shandy*.[45]

Although there is good reason to believe that Sterne's years at Cambridge were important ones for the novel, still they must not outweigh the thirty years of reading Sterne did after graduation. From the longer period of reading must have come many of the echoes, allusions, and references that fill *Tristram Shandy*. It can be recalled that the Widow Wadman, Uncle Toby, Walter Shandy, and Parson Yorick taken together had read a great many books, and that Tristram had read all of their books as well as scores of others. It cannot, of course, be assumed that Laurence Sterne had read everything he had Tristram Shandy mention, or that Tristram mentioned everything the author had read. Cross, has concluded, however, 'that to this formative period, the thirty-year reading one, we have a trustworthy though incomplete index in *Tristram Shandy* ".[46]

In *Illustrations of Sterne* Dr. John Ferriar, it can be recalled, presented fairly conclusive evidence of Sterne's borrowings from Rabelais, Beroalde, D'Aubigne, Cervantes, Bouchet, Bruscambille, Scarron, Swift, Gabriel John, Bacon, Blount, Montaigne, Bishop Hall, and Robert Burton.[47] Although Ferriar's *Illustrations* has proved to be a valuable aid to Sterne scholarship, it has been partly responsible for the emphasis given to Sterne's lighter reading and the near neglect of his more serious reading. Cross, for one example, in discussing Sterne's reading says that "first in the catalogue of books read by the Vicar of Sutton were three of the world's great humorists – Lucian, ... Rabelais, and ... Cervantes". He next mentions Bouchet, Bruscambille, Scarron, Ga-

---

[45] *Letters*, p. 87.
[46] *Life*, p. 139.
[47] See above, p. 20.

briel John, and Beroalde. Of Montaigne, Cross says: "Of these facetious writers Sterne classed Montaigne, who, though his work is of more serious import, wandered on whimsically, as everybody would have him, from one topic to another." Of Swift, he says: "To Sterne, Swift meant mainly *A Tale of a Tub,* a cock-and-bull story." [48]

Although Sterne's reading probably did comprise a considerable amount of the strange and out-of-the-way books that are mentioned in the novel, little notice has been given to the standard corpus of books [49] that furnished a part of the material for *Tristram Shandy.* There is, for example, the use of the Old Testament for the names for some of the characters. Great-Uncle Hammond, who had been hanged, bears some resemblance to the Haman of the Book of Esther.[50] Great-Aunt Dinah bears even more to the daughter of Jacob.[51] Equally unnoticed has been that not only Uncle Toby's name, "Tobias", but the sterile affair of Uncle Toby with the Widow Wadman and the story Trim told about his brother's courting the Jew's widow could have been taken from the Book of Tobit.[52]

Sterne could have taken several of Walter's curious beliefs from comparatively standard reading. Ferriar observed that "Sterne frequently had in view the *Tale of a Tub*", and that Swift's Dissertation on *Ears* probably contributed towards Sterne's digressions on *Noses*".[53] It can be recalled that Walter Shandy was anxious for his son to have a well-shaped nose. As for Walter's belief in the significance of names, Sterne could have found numerous instances in the Old Testament of the importance attached to names. And as for Walter's high regard for the name of Hermes Trismegistus, Sterne could easily have derived information concerning the strange manner in which Hermes had been wor-

---

[48] *Life*, p. 142.
[49] *Life*, p. 153.
[50] Esther, 6 : 8-10.
[51] Genesis, 30 : 37-41; 34 : 1-31.
[52] *The Apocrypha; or, Non-Canonical Books of the Bible. The King James Version* (ed.), Manuel Komroff (New York, Tudor Publishing Co., 1936), pp. 71-91.
[53] *Illustrations of Sterne*, I, p. 70.

shipped from such sources as Herodotus [54] and Thucydides. In fact, when Walter calls Hermes Trismegistus "the greatest of all earthly beings – the greatest king – the greatest lawgiver – the greatest philosopher – and the greatest priest",[55] the speech is very much like the description of Hermes Trismegistus in Bacon's dedication of the Advancement of Learning to King James:

> Your majesty standeth invested of that triplicity which in great veneration was ascribed to the greatest Hermes; the power and fortune of a king, the knowledge of a priest, and the learning and illumination of a philosopher.[56]

That Sterne might have derived the strange matter in *Tristram Shandy* from familiar books does not preclude his having found it in less familiar ones. And that he found many odd books in John Hall-Stevenson's library may very well be true. Peter Quennell draws an interesting picture of what Sterne saw there:

> Here in vellum-bound duodecimos or massive calf-clad folios, were those rare books of eccentric erudition or orthodox speculation in which Sterne most delighted, from the more fantastic fathers of the early church to sixteenth-century French divines who tempered the parade of scholastic learning with flights of licentious fancy. They encouraged the natural twists of his mind, and stocked his memory with a vast variegated accumulation he could draw upon at leisure.[57]

Although Peter Quennell apparently still believes that Sterne depended heavily upon Hall-Stevenson's books, Wilbur Cross some years ago modified the view of Sterne's dependency on them. Cross wrote:

> Writers on Sterne, repeating what was said a century ago have given a wide currency to the tradition that the humorist found and read at Skelton most of those strange volumes that go to the learning and adornment of *Tristram Shandy*. Though the tradition is far from the truth, Sterne's intimacy with Hall-Stevenson may have led him to

---

[54] Cf. *The Persian Wars*, trans. George Rawlinson (New York, Modern Library, 1947), I, p. 140.
[55] *Tristram Shandy*, pp. 283 f. Cf. *The History of the Peloponnesian War*, trans. Richard Crawley (New York, Dutton, Everyman's Library, 1950), pp. 229-230, 252.
[56] G. W. Kitchins (ed.), Everyman ed. (London and Toronto, J. M. Dent & Sons, 1915), p. 3.
[57] *The Profane Virtues*, p. 148.

reading curious books for one of his recreations in the long and obscure years at Sutton.[58]

The traditional insistence on John Hall-Stevenson's library as being more important to Sterne than his own, corresponded with the general denial of a purposeful Sterne. Cross has shown, however, that Sterne had access to several libraries besides that of his friend, and that Sterne built up a sizeable collection of his own from the book markets plentifully afforded by York.[59] At any rate, what books Sterne read in Hall-Stevenson's library, or for that matter, what books were there for him to read is, it seems, more conjectural than what books were in Sterne's own library. Cross argues that Sterne must have done most of his reading at home, where his own collection contained so many of the books whose contents appear one way or another in *Tristram Shandy*.[60]

The catalogue of Sterne's books, sold at auction in York a few months after his death, like the list that can be made from *Tristram Shandy*, is incomplete evidence of Sterne's reading. Fredman says of the collection: "There is no way of determining when Sterne collected his library – he increased it greatly by his purchase of seven-hundred books 'dog cheap' in 1761." [61] Ownership, furthermore, is no guarantee of reading. And "no man's reading is ever restricted to those volumes which appear upon his shelves", observed Hammond in noting the limited use that could be made of the catalogue for corroborative evidence of Sterne's having borrowed his sermon material from certain writers.[62]

Loosely, the catalogue lists several kinds of books. A number of them are in Greek and Latin; a few are in French; the majority are in English. It contains the standard works of philosophy, theology, literature, and science. And it includes Sterne's Chaucer, Erasmus, Montaigne, Rabelais, Cervantes, Shakespeare, Browne, Burton, Hobbes, Dryden, Locke, Swift, Pope, Addison, and Martin Scriblerus. Among them, can be found the writings of the

---

[58] *Life*, p. 138.
[59] *Life*, p. 139.
[60] *Ibid.*, p. 138.
[61] *Making of a Humorist*, p. 12.
[62] Lansing Van der Heyden Hammond, *Laurence Sterne's Sermons of Mr. Yorick* (New Haven, Yale University Press, 1948), pp. 8-9.

Ante-Nicean and Post-Nicean Fathers, Old Testament Apocrypha, the *Index Expurgatorius*, histories of strange customs and religions, medical writings, and treatises on mathematics, geography, and military science. The catalogue also contains books of more occult nature, for it lists the writings of the Cabala and of the mystics, and it includes three books on Freemasonry.

Whatever such a catalogue signifies, it makes it difficult to believe that Sterne picked up his erudition from Burton's *Anatomy of Melancholy* or from Chambers' *Universal Dictionary of Arts and Sciences*.[63]

With the exception of Dr. John Ferriar's discoveries of Sterne's indebtedness to "literary follies", the sources of *Tristram Shandy* were not taken seriously for many years. They were taken lightly perhaps because it was accepted that Sterne had skimmed from books or taken from Burton's *Anatomy of Melancholy* and Chambers' *Encyclopedia* what his erratic fancy had needed at the moment. Although it is now beginning to be accepted that Sterne was a more serious minded workman and *Tristram Shandy* is a more serious production than they were once considered to be, there is still the need to examine Sterne's sources and the use he made of them.

In some cases Sterne in borrowing what at first appears to be only *minutiae* brought along enough of its context to form an important thread in the novel. If it can be established, for example, that the Dinah of Genesis is the archetype of Tristram's Great-Aunt Dinah, the context of the original Dinah might then reveal the use Sterne made in *Tristram Shandy* of the word *"gentleman"* he included in the title of the work, *The Life and Opinions of Tristram Shandy, Gentleman*.

The first Dinah seriously imperiled the honour of the Biblical first family. Dinah, the daughter of Jacob, was ravished by the prince of an inferior people. The attempt of her brothers to restore her honor by persuading the prince and his people to be circumcised and then slaying them while they were sore brought infamy as well as dishonor to the family of Israel. Sterne had Tristram's Great-Aunt Dinah imperil the honor of the Shandy family by her

[63] *Life*, p. 152, note on Chamber's *Encyclopedia* controversy.

affair with the coachman.[64] It might have been the result of design instead of chance that caused Sterne to relate the effect her legacy was to have upon the Sterne family before Tristram was mangled by the falling window.[65] It might also have been more than a whimsical notion of Sterne that caused Susannah, who was responsible for the accident, to call it murder.[66]

It might not always be so easy as the hypothetical case of the defecting aunt appears to be to get a glimpse of Sterne's method by examining the original context of the allusions and references in *Tristram Shandy*. It should be possible, however, to find clues to his method among the books casually or seriously mentioned in the novel.

In fairness to book and author consideration must be given to the purposeful and efficient manner in which, despite difficulties, Sterne carried out the writing of *Tristram Shandy* and of the *Sentimental Journey* as well.

Although some of Sterne's biographers mention the troubles Sterne was having while he was writing *Tristram Shandy*, it appears that few of them find the difficulties as evidence of the resolute nature of Sterne, who wrote in spite of the obstacles. Cross has said of the composition of *Tristram Shandy:*

> It was a current story that Sterne had set about and continued *Tristram Shandy* as a relief to melancholy. "Every sentence", it was said, "had been conceived and written under the greatest heaviness of heart". Certain it is that the composition of his book was accompanied by domestic troubles that might have crushed a man of grave temperament, but they affected the light-hearted Yorick little if at all.[67]

Lodwick Hartley begins by saying "it mattered little that conditions in the Sutton parsonage were hardly propitious for literary production".[68] Peter Quennell appears to regard even less seriously than Hartley the difficulties Sterne encountered in writing *Tristram Shandy:*

---

[64] *Tristram Shandy*, pp. 65-66.
[65] *Ibid.*, p. 322.
[66] *Ibid.*, p. 326.
[67] *Life*, p. 195.
[68] *This is Lorence*, p. 76.

Its composition proceeded at a remarkably rapid pace. There are some writers – certainly not many – who, as cats are reputed to do, give birth with satisfaction; and, though Sterne was a diligent artist and laboriously revised his work, his pleasure in writing usually preponderated over the pains and difficulties.[69]

Quennell, a few pages later, wonders if one of Sterne's difficulties might not have been responsible for the writing of the novel:

Much has been written – with as little result – of the pathology of genius. To what extent can we attribute the activities of the brain to the activities of the body? Are there certain morbid conditions – the disease from which Sterne suffered being evidently one, syphilis in its suppressed stages perhaps another – that intensify the growth of a poetic gift? [70]

Sterne's trouble while he was writing the first two volumes of *Tristram Shandy* were sufficient, Hartley observes, "to break a man several times stronger than he".[71] "His mother died in May, 1759. Uncle Jacques followed in June of the same year." [72] Sterne's wife, according to Cross, sometime in that year was "suddenly stricken with palsy". She "went out of her senses, and 'fancied herself the Queen of Bohemia' ".[73] And to add to Sterne's troubles, "the sad condition of Mrs. Sterne affected the health of little Lydia, who had been ailing for some time, throwing the 'poor child into a fever' ".[74]

Sterne's financial condition, although not desperate, was not very satisfactory. Willard Connelly implies that the condition was not serious. After relating Sterne's disappointment over receiving nothing from the estate of Jacques Sterne, Connelly says of the author's difficulty in getting *Tristram Shandy* published:

To put the ictus on this mischance, Dodsley, before Jacques Sterne was cold in his coffin, replied with a list of hesitations. *Tristram*, as a single volume, would hardly attract publishers; ... The answer that the desperate Sterne made to these shortcomings was not to Dodsley.

[69] *Four Portraits*, pp. 150-151.
[70] *Ibid.*, p. 160.
[71] *This is Lorence*, p. 79.
[72] *Ibid.*
[73] *Life*, p. 196.
[74] *Ibid.*, p. 197.

The author plunged into revision, and at the same time he drove ahead, through the summer, with the indispensable second volume.[75]

There is also the matter of Sterne's not having received ecclesiastical preferment nor having distinguished himself by any other means. Hartley summarizes Sterne's condition as follows:

Although by the time he had reached forty-six Sterne had gained some local prominence, he seemed far from making his mark in the world. In his periods of melancholy and reflection this fact added materially to his discomfort. ... In short, he had neither health, worldly goods, position, nor happiness to show for the two decades.[76]

The nature of the seriousness of Sterne's troubles can be better realized if they are examined in slightly more detail. Although Hartley asserts that neither the death of Sterne's mother or uncle "could have caused him much sorrow", it is not altogether certain that his mother's death troubled Sterne as slightly as Hartley believed it did. Bitter recriminations had passed between Sterne and his mother when she, believing that he had married an heiress, had come with her daughter to make their home with him. He had refused "to oblige his wife to share her home with such uncomfortable relations-in-law as Mrs. Roger Sterne and her daughter".[77] According to John Croft, Sterne later "left his mother to die in the 'common gaol at York in a wretched condition, or soon after she was released' ".[78] How culpable Sterne's actions in the matter were, is hard to determine, but it seems that Quennell may have come close to the truth of what little effect the affair had on Sterne: "She passed out of his existence, leaving a permanent trace – perhaps a scar upon his conscience, certainly an odour of scandal from which, even posthumously, he never quite escaped." [79]

There is some reason to believe that Sterne and his mother had become reconciled only a short time before her death. Cross says:

After a long period of misunderstanding and estrangement, a reconciliation between mother and son had evidently been brought about

---

[75] *Laurence Sterne as Yorick* (London, Bodley Head, 1958), pp. 25-26.
[76] *This is Lorence*, p. 75.
[77] *The Making of a Humorist*, p. 89.
[78] *Life*, p. 109.
[79] *Four Portraits*, p. 145.

by her acceptance of the allowance that had been offered to her many years before. Blake, it would seem from a dark hint or two, had acted as mediator. For some purpose, at any rate, he was doling out money to York and sending accounts of it over to Sutton.[80]

Hartley says there is evidence of the reconciliation's having taken place in 1758, the year before Mrs. Roger Sterne's death.[81] Shaw and Connelly agree that Sterne had visited her in York in the middle of December in 1758.[82] There does not appear to be very good evidence that Sterne should have felt less grief for the death of his mother than any other man would have felt about his mother's death. There is some reason to believe that reconciliation after the long estrangement might have made Sterne's grief harder to bear.

As for the lack of grief for the death of Jacques Sterne, Hartley has remarked: "The fact that Dr. Sterne's death cut off Laurie's chance of inheriting his uncle's property produced a feeling of frustration. Sterne refused to wear the customary mourning." [83]

Sterne's being cut off from this inheritance was evidently the last of a lifetime of such exclusions from the benefits of being a Sterne. In the "Memoirs" he had somewhat proudly stated that his father was the grandson of Archbishop Sterne.[84] The Archbishop's son, Simon, had been sufficiently provident.

Simon Sterne married to his great good fortune, Mary Jacques, heiress to a large estate at Elvington, near the river Derwent.... Her brother Roger dying without issue, she succeeded as his heir to the lordship of Elvington. With £1800 Simon Sterne purchased Woodhouse, a large estate at Skircoat to the southwest of Halifax, with an Elizabethan mansion looking across the beautiful valley of the Calder.[85]

Laurence Sterne's uncle, Richard, the eldest son of Simon Sterne, inherited the estates of Elvington and Woodhouse. He was, said Cross, "most fortunate in his marriages", and grew to be the wealthiest of the Sternes, possessing besides his inherited estates,

[80] *Life*, pp. 124-125.
[81] *This is Lorence*, p. 50.
[82] *The Making of a Humorist*, p. 146; *Laurence Sterne as Yorick*, p. 25.
[83] *This is Lorence*, p. 79.
[84] See above, p. 34.
[85] *Life*, pp. 8-9.

THE MAN AND THE NOVELIST 51

lands at Ovendone and Hipporholme.[86] Laurence's other uncle, younger than Roger Sterne, was the Jacques Sterne who died in 1759, leaving his nephew nothing of his estate. It seems that he had been able to rise in the world by being "a worldly-wise ecclesiastic" who strove "for high place mainly for his own comfort and aggrandizement".[87] By the time he was forty, in 1735, "there was nothing further for him to ask for at present except a bishopric, but that could not be granted him".[88] By 1752 his income was "about £900 a year, as it appears from the memorandum" he submitted to the Duke of Newcastle.[89] Cross observed that the income "was really large for the eighteenth century".[90] It can be recalled that Simon Sterne had purchased the large estate of Woodhouse for only twice the amount.

Roger Sterne, however, had not taken the way to either wealth or distinction. Whether or not the military career that he chose for himself offered an opportunity for wealth and distinction, Roger Sterne got neither by being a soldier. Laurence Sterne wrote that his father married the sutler's daughter because he was indebted to the sutler. Neither Sterne's "Memoirs" nor the investigations of Cross had revealed that Roger Sterne ever bettered his condition much more than by that one act of relieving his indebtedness. Laurence Sterne stated in a letter to Jacques Sterne, that his mother "brought not one sixpence into the family".[91] It seems that Roger Sterne did little to improve his position in the army. Hartley says of Roger's military career: "Four years after his marriage he was listed as an ensign. His only advancement in rank came just before he died." [92]

In the "Memoirs" Laurence Sterne relates that by the time he was nine years old his family had spent three years in the homes of relatives: one with Roger's mother, another with a relative of

---

[86] *Ibid.*, p. 9.
[87] *Ibid.*, p. 37.
[88] *Ibid.*, p. 38.
[89] *Ibid.*, pp. 89-90.
[90] *Ibid.*, p. 90.
[91] *Life*, p. 108.
[92] *This is Lorence*, p. 7.

Agnes Sterne, and the third with a distant relative of Roger's. When Laurence was nine, his father placed him in school near Halifax, where he remained until he was eighteen, the same year his father died.[93] Hartley says that Laurence Sterne was placed in school near Halifax, "ostensibly because his Uncle Richard could keep him there under his surveillance".[94] Hartley also says that Richard "had received the child as a poor relation – with a solid sense of duty rather than with any scintilla of warmth or affection".[95]

M. R. B. Shaw says of the uncle-nephew relationship:

> His father's death left Laurence 'without one Shilling in the World' and, as it seemed at first 'without one Friend in it.' Moreover, as he shortly discovered, the money expended on School Education, Clothing, etc., for nine years together was a debt he would have to repay as soon as he was able.[96]

The friend Laurence found was Richard's son, likewise named Richard, who sent Laurence to Cambridge and provided for him thirty pounds a year.[97] Hartley speaks of Sterne's expenses at Cambridge as being "too scantily defrayed ..., with only thirty pounds a year".[98] Cross says of the expenses:

> Without running into debt there could have been for Sterne no luxuries nor suppers nor wine parties, such as were expected from youngsters from good families. Under the circumstances Sterne did exactly as one would expect of him: he borrowed money, from what source he does not say....[99]

Until Sterne graduated from Cambridge, his being a member of the Sterne family brought him a certain amount of shame as well as pride. After leaving Cambridge, he was helped by his Uncle Jacques to the living of Sutton on the Forest. Soon afterwards, Sterne was awarded the prebend of Givendale. And this second position had also been made possible by Jacques Sterne.[100]

[93] *Works*, V, 2-4.
[94] *This is Lorence*, p. 11.
[95] *Ibid.*, p. 12.
[96] *The Making of a Humorist*, p. 19.
[97] *Ibid.*, pp. 19-20.
[98] *This is Lorence*, p. 15.
[99] *Life*, p. 28.
[100] *Ibid.*, pp. 39-41.

Jacques Sterne's aiding Laurence was not altogether impelled by "a sense of duty to help along a member of the family who might come to something; but it is clear, in the light of subsequent events, that he mainly sought in his nephew a subservient tool for furthering his own ambitions".[101]

Whatever Jacques Sterne's motives might have been, it is evident that he did offer his nephew a way to become an important member of the Sterne family. And Laurence also gained the Prebendary of North Newbald by the help of his uncle. Whether or not Laurence should have quarrelled with his uncle, he did so and thereby lost the chance for further advancement and for inheriting any part of Jacques' estate.[102]

Although Laurence Sterne did not add to his fortune by marrying an heiress as Simon and Richard Sterne had done, or as Agnes Sterne believed that her son did, Laurence, it seems, had made a better marriage than Roger. Elizabeth Lumley brought her husband an income of "thirty or forty pounds a year". And it was due to her influence that Laurence received the additional living of Stillington.[103]

It does appear, however, that whatever the amount of wealth and distinction Sterne gained by the aid of his uncle and of his wife, it still was not enough to make him an important member of the Sterne family.

Laurence Sterne had tried to acquire both wealth and prestige. He had tried farming as one of the ways to more wealth. Sterne had "cultivated the glebe of his benefice; and not satisfied with this he purchased a neighboring farm".[104] Cross says that Laurence and Mrs. Sterne "kept a dairy farm at Sutton and had had seven milch cows".[105] Sterne made other purchases of land and other attempts at farming.

The same biographer states that "the high hopes, with which Sterne, having once purchased the land", and "set out on his

---

[101] *Ibid.*, p. 38.
[102] *Ibid.*, pp. 95, 195.
[103] *Ibid.*, pp. 54-55.
[104] *Ibid.*, p. 58.
[105] *Ibid.*

career as a farmer, ... were dashed to the ground" and "he cursed himself for his folly".[106]

Hartley says that "in the last year of his life Laurence summed up his disillusionment in a letter to Sir William Stanhope". Hartley quotes the letter:

I was once such a puppy myself, as to pare, and burn, and had my labour for my pains, and two hundred pounds out of pocket. – Curse on farming (said I) I will try if the pen will not succeed better than the spade. – The following up of that affair (I mean farming) made me lose my temper, and a cart load of turneps [sic] was (I thought) very dear at two hundred pounds....[107]

It also appears that Sterne attempted to win both wealth and prestige by pleasing others in authority besides his Uncle Jacques. He wrote a Latin sermon, a *Concio ad Clerum,* for Dean Fountaine to preach at Cambridge when the Dean went up for the degree of Doctor of Divinity, and he made himself useful to the Dean in other ways as well. For his efforts he was awarded two small commissaryships, but his benefactor could do nothing more for him without offending Jacques Sterne and the Archbishop.[108]

Out of the association with Fountaine, however, came Sterne's venture in political pamphleteering. He wrote *The History of a good Warm Watchcoat* to satirize the efforts of a Dr. Topham to gain a commissaryship for his son. Although Sterne permitted the pamphlet to be publicly burned because it was "offensive to the dignity of the Church",[109] it had a determining effect upon Sterne's future. "Having once discovered his talent", says Cross, "the country parson, then in his forty-sixth year, gave himself up to the exercise and delight of it for the rest of his life." [110]

In Sterne's forty-six years originated and had been cultivated many of the elements that enabled him to make of his writings something more than a pleasant exercise. Although there must have been a Sterne who "loved a jest in his heart", there also

---

[106] *Ibid.,* p. 61.
[107] *This is Lorence,* p. 36.
[108] *Life,* pp. 165-188.
[109] *Life,* p. 188.
[110] *Ibid.,* p. 189.

was the man of serious purposes. It cannot be denied that *Tristram Shandy* is a mirth-provoking book, but it scarcely can be called the autobiography of a whimsical author.

From the examination of Sterne's life made in this chapter Laurence Sterne appears to be somewhat different from the hero of his novel, and his relatives are not easily identified with Tristram's – Walter Shandy, Elizabeth Shandy, and Uncle Toby. Although Parson Yorick bears a recognizable resemblance to the author, Tristram has long been identified with Sterne because it has been difficult for the reader to separate the actual from the putative author.

The examination has also furnished some reasons to believe that Sterne was subjected to a great many sobering and disciplining influences, that his first ten years were not the happy, carefree ones they were once thought to have been, and that he did not idle away his time at public school and at the university as tradition has too much had it. It appears that before Sterne sat down to write his first novel he had read a great many books of more serious contents than those usually ascribed to him, and they too were responsible for the method of writing and the contents of *Tristram Shandy*.

Sterne's troubles at the time he began writing have been seen as evidence of the resolute character of the man who determined to write a good book as well as a witty one. His lifetime of exclusions from the benefits of being a Sterne has been seen as one that began to change for the better with the beginning of his novel writing career.

Although it has been difficult to separate the life of Sterne the man from that of the minister, I have thought it best to deal with that of the man in this chapter and with that of the minister in the next one.

III

THE MINISTER AND THE NOVELIST

From what we know of Sterne's education and reading, from the conventions and practice of preaching, and from what we can observe in Sterne's *Sermons of Mr. Yorick* and in *Tristram Shandy*, there are certain inferences which may reasonably be drawn concerning the effect Sterne's clerical vocation had on the writing of *Tristram Shandy*. In the present chapter three phases of Sterne's duties or obligations as minister, which were partly responsible for the way the novel was written, will be considered briefly. They are Sterne's reading, sermon preparation, and religious affirmations.[1]

In the preceding chapters it has been insisted upon that *Tristram Shandy* is a novel, not an autobiography. On the assumption, however, that the man as well as the artist writes the novel, it has also been maintained that the man and the work cannot be made too independent of each other. In this case the man was also a minister and had been an ordained one for twenty-two years before he became a novelist. It is also assumed that without the years in the ministry Sterne would have written a different novel.

To begin with, Sterne, while preparing for the ministry at Cambridge, read many books which later found their way into the novel. Margaret R. B. Shaw says of the reading at Cambridge:[2] "As one who was preparing to enter the church, Sterne would not only have followed the usual course of undergraduate studies,

---

[1] The influence of Sterne's profane reading will be examined in the next chapter.
[2] *The Making of a Humorist, 1713-1762* (London, The Richards Press, 1957), p. 113.

but would also have read the works of eminent theologians and divines."

In the twenty-two years that intervened between Sterne's ordination and writing, he continued and supplemented the reading begun at the university. *Tristram Shandy* contains a hint that Anglican clergymen were expected to be well-read men: Yorick's caustic comment that too many sermons were preached to show the extent of the preacher's reading indicates that such was the general case.[3] And Cross says that "as a divine Sterne knew well the religious literature expected of him".[4]

Sterne's reading related to his ministry, may be grouped roughly as follows: the Bible, the writings of the fathers, the sermons of the seventeenth- and eighteenth-century divines, and the writings of the "polemical divines" of his own day.

Although Sterne might have read his Bible as often and as closely without his being a clergyman, his being one made it imperative that he read it. According to Garat, Sterne told Suard that the Bible was the book he read the most.[5] Kenneth MacLean, while arguing the dominating influence of Locke on Sterne, nevertheless concedes that Sterne read the Bible more than he read Locke.[6]

Patristic literature must also have been a part of his reading. According to Lecky the writings of the Fathers were regarded by the Church of England "as almost equal in authority to those of the inspired writers ... It had ever been the pride of the great divines of the seventeenth century that they were the most profound students of the Patristic writings".[7] Evidence of Sterne's having some knowledge of the writings of the Fathers can be seen in the several references in *Tristram Shandy* to St. Thomas Aquinas, Pentenus, Tertullianus, St. Jerome, St. Ambrose, St.

[3] *Tristram Shandy*, p. 317.
[4] *Life*, p. 153.
[5] Wilbur L. Cross, *The Life and Times of Laurence Sterne*, 3rd ed. (New Haven, Yale University Press, 1929), p. 302.
[6] *John Locke and English Literature of the Eighteenth Century* (New Haven, Yale University Press, 1936), p. 1.
[7] C. Wright Mills (ed.), W. E. C. Lecky, *History of the Rise and Influence of the Spirit of Rationalism in Europe* (New York, George Brazilier, 1955), I, pp. 171 f.

Gregory of Nanzianus, and St. Clement of Alexandria.[8] The catalogue of Sterne's library, previously mentioned, lists also the works of Eusebius (No. 336), Lactantius (359), Melancthon (473), and Origen (744).[9]

We can believe that Sterne read the commentaries of those closer to his own time. Lansing Van der Hammond, who has closely examined Sterne's sermons, demonstrates how greatly Sterne was indebted for the material that composed his sermons to some of the seventeenth- and early eighteenth-century divines: Blair, Bentley, Clarke, Foster, Hall, Leightenhouse, Rogers, Swift, Stillingfleet, Tillotson, Waterland, and Young.[10]

It is with Sterne as with many other writers, difficult to determine whether some of the Biblical elements in his work came from this close reading of the Scriptures or from the "theology in his background".[11] In Sterne's case the theological controversies of his day furnished a convenient source of material. Lecky says of William Warburton, Bishop of Gloucester, who after the novel first appeared became Sterne's patron: "Warburton was the leader of the Anglican clergy in abandoning Patristic miracles", and in establishing "the peculiar character and evidence of the miracles recorded by the evangelists".[12] George Sherburn calls Warburton the "leader of a school of reasoners", who, in contrast with the calmer Hume, "were excitingly abusive or paradoxically or ironically entertaining".[13] Sterne in 1760 was familiar enough with Warburton's *Divine Legation of Moses* that when he wrote to Garrick for an introduction to Warburton, he spoke of the bishop as "the author – God bless him! – of the *Divine Legation*".[14] In 1766 Sterne again referred to Warburton's work. He has Tristram write in the final volume of *Tristram Shandy*

---

[8] *Tristram Shandy*, pp. 58, 161, 414, 458, 467, and 583.
[9] *A Facsimile Reproduction of a Unique Catalogue of Laurence Sterne's Library*. Introduction by Charles Whibley (London, Tregaskis, 1930).
[10] *Laurence Sterne's Sermons of Mr. Yorick* (New Haven, Yale University Press, 1948), p. 10.
[11] Nathalia Wright, *Melville's Use of the Bible* (Durham, North Carolina, Duke University Press, 1949), p. 16.
[12] Lecky, *History of Rationalism*, p. 173.
[13] *A Literary History of England*, p. 1083.
[14] *Life*, p. 210.

that he hopes his own book will "swim down the gutter of time with the *Divine Legation of Moses* and with *Swift's Tale of a Tub*".[15]

Certain elements in *Tristram Shandy* – the names of some of the characters, the going back to the beginning to relate the life of the hero, the odd bits of learning, and the strange theories of Walter Shandy – can be found in the books, which there is reason to believe Sterne read as a minister.

The names of some of the characters in the novel can be found in the Old Testament and in the Apocrypha, and in a few cases Sterne's characters resemble the original bearers of the names. Attention has been called to the ways in which Great-Aunt Dinah resembles the daughter of Jacob and to those in which Uncle Toby was a model of chastity like Tobias of the apocryphal Book of Tobit.[16] It can be added that Uncle Toby's burying Le Fever was not unlike Tobias' burying the slain of his people.

For Walter's servant, Obadiah, there is the minor prophet Obadiah, who inveighed against the Edomites, the children of Esau. Sterne's Obadiah is a curious inversion of the Scriptural one. He is an unwitting, but nonetheless active, agent who works against the house of Shandy: He breeds Walter's mare to a jack, hinders the birth of Tristram by running down Dr. Slop and by tying the bag of obstetrical instruments and causing the doctor to cut his thumb. The Shandies might well have joined the physician in reading the curse of Bishop Ernulphus against Obadiah. And Obadiah, finally, damns the potency of the Shandy bull, which apparently symbolized the potency, or the lack of it, of Walter, Uncle Toby, and Tristram. Furthermore, when symbols are all about, Obadiah as the hairy man who has begotten a hairy child looks very much like an ectypal Esau.

The name of Trismegistus, although the hero was accidentally prevented from being so christened, is nonetheless an important one in the novel. There was an abundance of available sources of it; Sterne could have found references to Hermes Trismegistus in

---

[15] *Tristram Shandy*, p. 610.
[16] See above, p. 43.

many of the more secular books,[17] and there were references to him in much of the religious literature. St. James Stack in the *Encyclopedia of Religion and Ethics* says that references to him can be found in the writings of the Fathers – in that of Clement of Alexandria, Lactantius, Cyril, Stobeus, and Philo Judaeus.[18] It might be added that Augustine devoted two chapters in the *City of God* to "the Egyptian Hermes, whom they call Trismegistus",[19] and that Arnobius defended Christianity against the "followers of Plato and Pythagoras".[20] These writings are referred to in *Tristram Shandy*, and they are in the catalogue of Sterne's books sold at auction.[21]

Sterne could also have found a discussion of Hermes Trismegistus and of the Hermetic Books in Warburton's *Divine Legation*. Warburton argues that the books were forgeries made by the Platonists and the Pythagoreans against the Christians, and counter forgeries made by the Christians.[22]

D. W. Jefferson has said of the way Sterne began *Tristram Shandy:* "The entire structure of the work depends on the fact that the starting-point of the novel is not Tristram's birth but his begetting." [23] Tristram explains his reasons for beginning it in such a fashion:

Right glad I am, that I have begun the history of myself in the way I have done; and that I am able to go on tracing everything in it, as *Horace* says, *ab Ovo*.

Horace, I know, does not recommend this fashion altogether: but

[17] Cf. Whibley, *op. cit.*, and see above, p. 44.
[18] James Hastings (ed.), *Encyclopedia of Religion and Ethics* (New York, Charles Scribner's Sons), VI, pp. 626-629.
[19] Whitney J. Oates (ed.), *Basic Writings of St. Augustine* (New York, Random House, 1948), II, 23 f., 126-132.
[20] "The Seven Books Against the Heathen", in *The Ante-Nicean Fathers*, ed. Philip Schaff (New York, Christian Literature Co., 1887-1894), VI, p. 439.
[21] Cf. Whibley, *op. cit.*, and see above, p. 46.
[22] William Warburton, *The Divine Legation of Moses Demonstrated, on the Principles of a Religious Deist* (London, Printed for F. Gyles, 1738), III, p. 403 f.
[23] " 'Tristram Shandy' and Its Tradition", in *From Dryden to Johnson, The Pelican Guide to English Literature*, ed. Boris Ford (Hammondsworth, Middlesex, Penguin Books Ltd., 1957), p. 339.

that gentleman is speaking only of an epic poem or a tragedy; – (I forget which) – besides if it was not so, I should beg Mr. Horace's pardon – for in writing what I have set about, I shall confine myself neither to his rules, nor to any man's rules that ever lived.[24]

But Sterne could have found a number of examples in the Old and the New Testament of stories that began with an account of the circumstances attending the begetting. One can recall that Isaac, Joseph, and Samson were begotten under unusual conditions, and that their histories begin with an account of their begetting.

Walter Shandy's belief about the homunculus can be found among the books Sterne read as a minister. Thayer, in *Laurence Sterne in Germany*, considered that "Goethe's *Homunculus* had been suggested to the master partly by a reading of Paracelsus and partly by Sterne's meditations".[25] Although the matter of Goethe's indebtedness to Paracelsus suggests that Sterne likewise might have been indebted to the alchemist, Sterne, however, could have derived the idea from a number of other sources. Dampier says of the general view of embryology that was held before Aristotle:

In general embryology his [Aristotle's] ideas mark an important advance Earlier views, possibly derived from Egypt, regarded the father as the only real parent, the mother providing merely a home and nourishment for the embryo. Such beliefs were widespread and largely underlay patriarchal customs both in the ancient and the modern world.[26]

A convenient source for the idea would have been the Old and the New Testaments, in which many references are made to the seed of Abraham, the children of Abraham, the sons of Jacob, the children of Israel, the tribe of Judah, and the root of Jesse.

The Patristic writings contain the teaching that the male is solely responsible for generation: Methodius, an Antenicean Father, argued that begetting was like the removal of the rib from

---

[24] *Tristram Shandy*, p. 7 f.
[25] Harvey Waterman Thayer (New York, Columbia University Press, 1905), p. 101.
[26] William Cecil Dampier, *A History of Science and its Relation with Philosophy and Religion*, 4th ed. (Cambridge University Press, 1949), p. 84.

Adam in the creation of Eve.[27] "Augustine, put forward the theory of our seminal existence", says E. J. Bicknell, "as Levi existed in the loins of Abraham".[28] Aquinas in the *Summa Theologica* stated that "whatever is transmitted by the way of human origin is caused by the semen".[29]

In turning to Sterne's sermon preparation, one can notice that L. H. V. Hammond, the editor of *Sterne's Sermons of Mr. Yorick*, has listed several features shared by the novels and the first four published volumes of the sermons:

> Here one constantly encounters most of these features which made *Tristram Shandy* and *A Sentimental Journey* so distinctive; the same ability to conceive dialogue, create characters, and furnish a scene with sharply etched background; the digressions and eccentricities of punctuation; the obvious delight in alternately shocking and then moving people to tears by the soft and delicate states of emotion; and the whole, clothed in a style as subtle and flexible in texture and showing as great an economy of means as any that English prose had yet known.[30]

Hammond produces evidence that Sterne, early in his career, had made use of the published sermons of Swift, Hall, Tillotson, Clarke, Blair, Young, and others in preparing his own sermons. He does not believe however that Sterne acted as did Sir Roger de Coverley's curate, who added no more than "a good aspect and a clear voice to proven material".[31] He finds much to admire in Sterne's skill in paraphrasing the original material, in adding to it and in making jointures. He says of one of the early sermons, "The Temporal Advantages of Religion", "Various fragments were joined together so skillfully that, when combined, they read as though one man had written them all, and at one time – truly an amazing performance." [32]

[27] Alexander Roberts and James Donaldson (eds.), *The Ante-Nicene Fathers*, II, p. 271 f.
[28] "The Fall", in *Essays Catholic and Critical* (Macmillan, 1926), p. 214.
[29] *Basic Writings of St. Thomas*, ed. Anton C. Pegis (New York, Random House, 1944), p. 664.
[30] Lansing H. Van der Hammond, *Sterne's Sermons of Mr. Yorick* (New Haven, Yale University Press, 1948), p. 45.
[31] Cf. Gregory Smith (ed.), *The Spectator*, Everyman ed. (London, J. M. Dent & Sons, 1933), I, No. 106.
[32] Hammond, *op. cit.*, p. 78.

Hammond reasons, that it was some years later when Sterne discovered his own powers of sermon preparation: "His conception of sermon writing had undergone a change... He was no longer content to copy what had been written by others; he now preferred to see for himself what could be done with a text." [33] Hammond, furthermore, makes the interesting observation that Sterne began then to develop the Shandean style of writing:

Sterne began experimenting: phrases were refashioned and given greater effectiveness; new ways were found for heightening the dramatic or emotional possibilities of a scene, character sketches became sharply etched.... And "Shandyism" ... manifested itself at least a decade before the opening chapters of Tristram Shandy were set down on paper.[34]

The twenty-two years Sterne spent in preparing sermons would appear to be the most likely time for Sterne to have learned how to read and explicate a text. Somewhere and at some time he had learned enough about reading and explicating to present Walter Shandy in the act of misreading:

... As the dialogue was of Erasmus, my father soon came to himself, and read it over and over again with great application, studying every word and every syllable of it thro' and thro' in its most strict and literal interpretation, – he could still make nothing of it, that way. Maybe there is more meant than is said in it quoth my father. – Learned men, brother Toby, don't write dialogues upon long noses for nothing. – I'll study the mystic and allegoric, – here is room to turn a man's self in, brother.
My father read on.
. . . .
Nature had been prodigal in her gifts to my father beyond measure, and had sown the gifts of verbal criticism as deep within him, as she had done the seeds of all other knowledge, so that he had got out his penknife, and was trying experiments upon the sentence, to see if he could not scratch some better sense into it. – I've got within a single letter, brother *Toby*, cried my father, of Erasmus, his mystic meaning. – You are near enough, brother, replied my uncle, in all conscience. – Pshaw! cried my father, scratching on, – I might as well be seven miles off. – I've done it, said my father, snapping his fingers. – See

---

[33] *Ibid.*, p. 64.
[34] *Ibid.*

my dear brother *Toby,* how I have mended the sense. – But you have marr'd a word, replied my uncle Toby. – My father put on his spectacles, – bit his lip, – and tore out the page in a passion.[35]

One does not have to dig so carefully into the account of Walter's reading as Walter dug into the dialogue of Erasmus to see that Sterne had definite ideas about reading. Tristram shows that material should be read as it is written, not as the reader would have it rewritten; that passages have their meanings in context, not in isolation; and that a work depends upon all of its parts. Walter, by marring a word, had rendered a page useless; by tearing out a page, he had rendered the whole work useless.

That Sterne as a minister knew how to read and explicate a text can be seen in one of his sermons, "Search the Scriptures". Sterne deals with the scriptural account of the reconciliation of Joseph and his Brethren:

And Joseph said unto his brethren, I am Joseph; doth my father yet live? and his brethen could not answer him; for they were troubled at his presence.

. . . .

And he fell upon his brother Benjamin's neck, and wept; and Benjamin wept upon his neck.

Moreover, he kissed all his brethren, and wept upon them; and after that his brethren talked with him.[36]

Sterne argues the superiority of the scriptures over profane works, and he cites the silence of the brothers of Joseph as the paradoxical method of making a statement by refraining from saying anything:

When Joseph makes himself known, and weeps aloud upon the neck of his dear brother Benjamin, that all the house of Pharaoh heard him. – On all sides, there immediately issues a deep and solemn silence infinitely more eloquent than anything else could have been substituted in its place. . . . For when such a variety of contrary passions broke in upon them – what tongue was able to utter their hurried and distracted thoughts? – When remorse, surprise, shame, joy, and gratitude, struggled together in their bosoms, how uneloquently would their lips have performed their duty? – How unfaithfully their tongues have spoken the language of their hearts? In this case silence was

[35] *Tristram Shandy,* pp. 229 f.
[36] Genesis 45 : 1-3, 14-15.

truly eloquent and natural, and tears expressed what oratory was incapable of.

. . . .

I shall close with an excellent collect from our church:
Blessed Lord, who has caused all Holy Scriptures to be written for our learning, – grant that we may in such wise hear them, read, mark, and inwardly digest them.[37]

Sterne by the method he used in dealing with the account in Genesis of Joseph and Benjamin indicates not only some proficiency in reading, marking, and inwardly digesting but also a certain amount of ability in judging literary excellence. He of course could have, and probably did, learn from Longinus of the art possessed by the scriptures. In the same discourse he calls attention to "that glorious description which Moses gives of the creation of the heavens and the earth, which Longinus, the best critic the eastern world ever produced, was so justly taken with".[38] Sterne might also have learned the important lesson more thoroughly from the years of reading the Bible and have used what he had learned first in sermon making and later on in novel writing.

There is some evidence in *Tristram Shandy* that Sterne had learned something of the art of leaving certain things unsaid, which he had praised in the Biblical acount of Joseph and his brethren. Tristram concludes the Le Fever scene in the following manner:

Nature instantly ebb'd again, – the film returned to its place, – the pulse fluttered – stopp'd – went on – throbb'd – stopp'd again – moved – shall I go on? – No.[39]

Several other instances can be found in *Tristram Shandy* of Sterne's leaving some things unsaid. How effective the device is, can be observed in the skirmish between Dr. Slop and Uncle Toby:

Sir replied Dr. Slop, it would astonish you to know what improvements we have made in late years in all branches of obstetrical knowl-

---

[37] *Sermons II, Sterne's Works*, VII, p. 232.
[38] *Ibid.*, p. 230.
[39] *Tristram Shandy*, p. 246.

edge, but particularly in that one single point of the safe and expeditious extraction of the *foetus*, which has received such lights, that for my part (holding up his hands) I declare I wonder how the world has — I wish, quoth my uncle *Toby*, you had seen what prodigious armies we had in Flanders.[40]

Sterne, instead of describing Dr. Slop's reaction, ends the chapter with Uncle Toby's remark.

When Sterne began writing sermons, he would have found that whatever he preached had to be couched fairly well within a structural limit. The sermon has a relatively uniform structure and a certain amount of veneration attached to the form.[41] Sterne as a beginning minister would have found it safer to write his sermon and then deliver it.[42] The sermon also imposed certain conventions. Although delivery was relatively stylized, immediacy could not be disregarded; it should appear to be spoken, not read aloud.[43] That Sterne to an unusual degree could give the illusion of unpremeditated speech can be tested by a short extract from the sermon, "Philanthropy Recommended":

AND BY CHANCE THERE CAME DOWN A CERTAIN PRIEST! — Merciful God! that a teacher of thy religion should ever want humanity — or that a man whose head might be full of the one, should ever have a heart void of the other! This, however, was the case before us.[44]

One can get the same kind of illusion by reading the dialogue in *Tristram Shandy* singled out for admiration by Herbert Read:

Prithee, Trim! said he taking up his pipe again, — bring me a pen and ink: Trim brought paper also.

Take a full sheet — Trim! said my uncle Toby, making a sign at the same time to sit down close to him at the table. The corporal obeyed — placed paper directly before him — took a pen and dipped it in the ink.

[40] *Ibid.*, p. 144.
[41] Richard F. Jones, "The Attack on Pulpit Oratory in the Restoration", *JEGP*, XXX (1934), pp. 188-217. See also F. N. Robinson's note to the *Pardoner's Prologue*, in *The Poetical Works of Chaucer*, Cambridge ed. (Boston, Houghton Mifflin Co., 1933), p. 834.
[42] "Preaching", *Encyclopedia of Religion and Ethics*, ed. James Hastings (New York, Scribner, 1931), X, p. 217.
[43] "Preaching", *Dictionary of the Bible*, ed. James Hastings (New York, Charles Scribner's Sons, 1947).
[44] *Sterne's Works*, IV, p. 24.

– She has a thousand virtues, Trim! said my uncle Toby –
Am I to set them down, and please your honour? quoth the corporal.
But they must be taken in their ranks, replied my uncle Toby –
. . . .
Because, added the corporal, lowering his voice, and speaking very distinctly as he assigned the reason –
The knee is such a distance from the main body – whereas the groin, your honour knows, is upon the very *curtain* of the *place*.
My uncle Toby gave a long low whistle – but in a note which could scarce be heard across the table.
The corporal had advanced too far to retire – in three words he told the rest –
My uncle Toby laid down his pipe as gently upon the fender, as if it had been spun from the unravelling of a spider's web –
– Let us go to my brother Shandy's, said he.[45]

After citing the passage from *Tristram Shandy*, Read says of Sterne's writing: "How rarely does the critic see beyond the man Sterne to the triumph of his style – the greatest triumph (for flexibility, for fluidity, for delicacy) in the whole range of our prose."[46] He, furthermore, sees Sterne's accomplishment as the result of many years of preparatory writing. Although Read does not specify the nature of Sterne's preparation, sermon writing must surely have been an important part of it.

We know, for example, how long Sterne laboured to perfect his easy style ... how rarely does the critic see beyond the man Sterne to the triumph of his style – the greatest triumph (for flexibility, for fluidity, for delicacy) in the whole range of our prose.[47]

It can be added to Read's encomium that Sterne's prose was soon recognized as sounding well when read aloud. Howes says of the inclusions from Sterne in Enfield's *Speaker*, published in London in 1777: "Enfield's *Speaker*, a popular text on elocution, had ten selections from Sterne, a number exceeded only by those from Shakespeare."[48] It might be added that a speaking voice appears to

---

[45] Quoted in Herbert Read, *English Prose Style* (New York, Henry Holt and Company, 1928), pp. 163-164. See also *Tristram Shandy*, pp. 641-642.
[46] *English Prose Style*, p. 166.
[47] *Ibid.*
[48] Alan B. Howes, *Yorick and the Critics; Sterne's Reputation in England, 1760-1868* (New Haven, Yale University Press, 1958), pp. 51-52.

come through whenever it is read silently. To modify Coleridge's praise of "Venus and Adonis", we seem to see and hear everything; and, at the same time, we hear a voice that tells us everything. If it can be admitted that this quality of Sterne's prose exists, it is reasonable to suppose that the result, in part at least, of the years Sterne spent in writing sermons was to create the illusion he was not reading aloud but was speaking his thoughts as they came to him. To his practice, of course, must be added his genius.

Sterne's sermons reveal that before the minister began writing a novel he had developed a facility for extracting startling meanings from the Scriptures. Dr. Johnson was of the opinion that in Sterne's sermons was to be found only "the froth from the cup of salvation".[49] Thomas Gray felt that Sterne was "often tottering on the verge of laughter and ready to throw his periwig in the face of the audience". But Gray also said that the sermons were "most proper for the pulpit" and that they showed "a very strong imagination and a sensible heart".[50] William Cowper called Sterne "a great master of the pathetic", and he further observed, "if that or any other species of rhetoric could renew the human heart and turn it from the power of Satan unto God, I know no writer better qualified to make proselytes to the cause of virtue".[51]

Whether or not the startling interpretations were made to serve a rhetorical or a more serious purpose, the sermons did provide a certain amount of exercise in creating what was new and surprising. In one, "The Pharisee and the Publican", he found the Pharisee to be as serious and as honest in his prayer as the Publican was in his.[52] In another, 'The Prodigal Son", Sterne blamed the father for permitting the inexperienced young man to make the Grand Tour without a wise traveling companion.[53] In still another, "Inquiry after Happiness", he called Solomon one of

[49] *Yorick and the Critics*, p. 10.
[50] Paget Toynbee and Leonard Whibley (eds.), *Correspondence of Thomas Gray* (Oxford, Clarendon Press, 1935), II, p. 681.
[51] Thomas Wright (ed.), *Correspondence of William Cowper* (London, Hoddor and Stoughton, 1904), I, p. 64 f.
[52] *Works*, VI, p. 76.
[53] *Ibid.*, VI, p. 76.

the greatest in a long line of "reformed sensualists".[54] In the sermon included in *Tristram Shandy*, as well as in the *Sermons of Mr. Yorick*, "The Abuses of Conscience Considered", Sterne made the word, "trust", synonymous with "doubt". The text, "We trust we have a good conscience", rendered in such a fashion was indeed enough to cause Dr. Slop to believe the preacher was going to abuse the Apostle.[55]

In *Tristram Shandy* Sterne made a great deal of use of the unexpected. At the conclusion of the first volume of it he boasted of his ability:

What these perplexities of my Uncle *Toby* were, – 'tis impossible for you to guess; – if you could, – I should blush, – not as a relation, – not as a man, – nor even as a woman, – but I should blush as an author; inasmuch as I set no small store by myself upon this very account, that my reader has never yet been able to guess at anything.[56]

A Sentimental Journey contains an excellent use of the unexpected. When Yorick sees a caged starling that has been taught to speak, Sterne has the starling say what is not expected but what is the most appropriate for the starling to say – "I want out!" There is a fittingness in Sterne's taking a starling for his crest, not for the symbol of thwarted longing in every soul to escape, but for an indication of the peculiar quality of the pattern of his interpretations.

The sermons reveal however that the pattern of Sterne's wit was not static enough to make prediction of what he was going to say easy. Somewhere Sterne had learned the trick of establishing the reasonableness of a novel interpretation, only to overthrow it with another equally novel. After establishing the second, he would overthrow it with a third, and so on. In the sermon, "The Levite and the Concubine",[57] he began by condemning the sin of concubinage. He next excused the Levite because of the lawless times: "There was no king in those days, and each man was a law unto himself." But, after he had established the right of free-

[54] *Ibid.*, VI, p. 7.
[55] *Tristram Shandy*, p. 123.
[56] *Ibid.*, p. 80.
[57] *Works*, VI, pp. 204-215.

dom, he condemned the woman for exercising her freedom: she left the Levite and went a whoring. Finally, after having made a case against her, he overturned it by applauding the Levite's forgiving nature, which caused him to follow and reclaim her.

Sterne later sported somewhat after the same fashion with the readers of *Tristram Shandy*. At the end of the nineteenth chapter of the first volume Tristram pities his father for having a child named "Tristram":

> If ever malignant spirit took pleasure, or busied itself in traversing the purposes of mortal man – it must have been here; – and if it was not necessary I should be born before I was christened, I would this moment give the reader an account of it.[58]

In the next chapter Sterne chides the reader for not being able to read as well as he should:

> How could you, Madam, be so inattentive in reading the last chapter? I told you in it *that my mother was not a papist.* – Papist! You told me no sucht thing, Sir. ... I do insist upon it, that you immediately turn back, that is as soon as you get to the next full stop, and read the whole chapter over again.
> . . . .
> And did you not observe the passage on the second reading, which admits the inference? Not a word like it! Then, Madam, be pleased to ponder well the last line but one of the chapter, where I take upon me to say, "It was *necessary* I should be born before I was christened." Had my mother, Madam, been a Papist, that consequence did not follow.[59]

After having shown the reader what had not been observed, Sterne next proceeds to startle the reader again by giving a reason other than carelessness for the reader's missing the line:

> This self-same vile pruriency for fresh adventure in all things, has got so strongly into our habits and humours, – and so wholly intent are we upon satisfying the impatience of our concupiscence that way, that nothing but the gross and more carnal parts of a composition will go down. . . .[60]

[58] *Tristram Shandy*, p. 56.
[59] *Ibid.*, pp. 56-57.
[60] *Ibid.*, p. 57.

Tristram Shandy contains more than a little of this kind of thing. Tristram after pretending to write with perfect freedom, finds it strange that Walter Shandy could be eloquent without any familiarity with the authorities on rhetoric:

> And yet, 'tis strange, he had never read *Cicero* nor *Quintilian de Oratore*, nor *Isocrates*, nor *Aristotle*, nor *Longinus* amongst the ancients; – nor *Vossius*, nor *Skoppius*, nor *Ramus*, nor *Farnaby* amongst the moderns; – and what is more astonishing, he had never in his whole life the least spark of subtilty struck into his mind, by one single lecture upon *Crackenthorp* or *Burgerdicius*, or any Dutch logician or commentator; – he knew not so much as in what the difference of an argument *ad ignorantiam*, and an argument *ad hominem* consisted. . . .[61]

He furthermore assures the reader that he has been told all about the characters. But Mrs. Shandy, whom he presents as never asking a question, asks what are perhaps the most important questions in the book: Did Walter Shandy forget to wind the clock? Was Uncle Toby in love with the Widow Wadman? And what is *Tristram Shandy* all about? Uncle Toby is presented as one who reverences God and dearly loves his fellow creatures. After Walter had insulted Uncle Toby's hobby horse, the old gentleman "looked up into [Walter's] face with a countenance spread over with so much good nature – so placid – so fraternal; – so inexpressibly tender towards him; it penetrated [Walter] to the heart".[62] The same gentle Uncle Toby is later to cut off the tops of the ancestral jackboots,[63] to leave his inheritance to Trim,[64] and to trap Walter into choosing Le Fever's ignorant son for Tristram's tutor.[65] Uncle Toby piously enough sees the world as it has pleased God to make it. "There is no cause but one, replied my uncle Toby, – why one man's nose is longer than another's, but because that God pleases to have it so." [66] When Trim asserts that the soldiers who died bravely would go to Heaven for it,

---

[61] *Ibid.*, p. 52.
[62] *Ibid.*, p. 115.
[63] *Ibid.*, p. 205.
[64] *Ibid.*, p. 276.
[65] *Ibid.*, p. 432.
[66] *Ibid.*, p. 240.

Uncle Toby nods to Yorick and says, "Trim is right".[67] It is indeed surprising when Uncle Toby adds blasphemy to the resolution that Le Fever should not die: "Do what we can for him, said *Trim*, maintaining his point, – the poor soul will die; – He shall not die, by *G*—, cried my uncle Toby." Sterne then adds another surprise as he had done in the sermon of the Levite and the Concubine. "The ACCUSING SPIRIT which flew up to Heaven's chancery with the oath, blush'd as he gave it in; – and the RECORDING ANGEL as he wrote it down, dropp'd a tear upon the word, and blotted it out forever." [68]

Thus far the assumption has been that Sterne's education, reading, and sermon preparation had a favorable effect upon the writing of *Tristram Shandy*. But in turning to the minister's convictions, or affirmations of convictions, one cannot be sure that Sterne's anti-Catholic bias was always helpful to the novelist.

Hammond says of the anti-Catholic sentiment in Sterne's sermons that "instead of arguing the matter soberly, as so many others had done, pointing out the errors and inconsistencies in such dogmas, Sterne contented himself with denunciations and abuse." [69] Wilbur L. Cross has found that Sterne transferred his animus toward the Roman Catholic from his preaching to the novel, and he has found a direct connection between Sterne's preaching and the handling of Dr. Slop in *Tristram Shandy*:

> Sterne's frightful caricature of an able and learned antiquary is unexplainable without reference to the fierce religious passions awakened by the events of 1745, when every church, from the cathedral of St. Peter's to the remotest parish, rang with denunciations of Rome and all her ways.... His own [Sterne's] sermons, such as without doubt belong to this period might have been written, so far as their tone is concerned, either by the archbishop or the archdeacon. The point of difference is but one of style. Neither of the men in higher places defined Popery, with reference to penances and indulgences, quite so neatly as Sterne as when he called it "a pecuniary system, well contrived to operate upon their passions and weakness, whilst their pockets are o'picking". He preached eloquently against the Mass and its mummeries, auricular confession, the arts of the Jesuits, and

---

[67] *Ibid.*, p. 380.
[68] *Ibid.*, p. 425.
[69] Hammond, *Laurence Sterne's Sermons of Mr. Yorick*, p. 94.

"the cruelties, murders, rapine, and bloodshed" that ever accompanied Rome in her history.[70]

Despite the fact that Cross calls the presentation of Dr. Slop, "a frightful caricature", one can see that Sterne allows the doctor to have several triumphs. Although Obadiah runs him down with the coach horse, the midwife is put over him, he cuts his hand in opening the green baize bag, and has some uncomfortable moments trying to explain to Uncle Toby how the obstetrical instruments work, he nevertheless curses Obadiah with the curse of Bishop Ernulphus, tears the skin off Uncle Toby's hand with the forceps, ousts the midwife, and delivers the infant Tristram.

The attacks on Catholicism in the way Sterne deals with the Catholic Doctor are not particularly vicious. The parallel between the doctor's reliance on obstetrical instruments to effect delivery and on instruments of the church to enforce salvation is perhaps the most severe. "The Inquisition has its uses." Generally, Sterne makes Dr. Slop a good fighter, and one who is able to defend his religious convictions, as well as his medical practice, against the attacks of Walter Shandy and Uncle Toby. He has some difficulty in answering Uncle Toby's guileless queries. He is, for example, nonplussed by the innocent question: "How many sacraments are there? I can never remember." And he is further discomfited when Uncle Toby apologizes for not understanding the explanation. But he fares better against Walter Shandy's intentional attacks, for he expects them and he is prepared to meet them. Furthermore, when he is forced to listen to the Protestant sermon he comes much nearer to hearing his belief concerning conscience preached than is ordinarily recognized, for Yorick's "Abuses of Conscience Considered" does not give the individual conscience much authority.[71]

The presentation of Dr. Slop is a milder attack on Catholicism than some of the others within the novel – the comments of the docteurs of the Sorbonne, the curse of Bishop Ernulphus, the

---

[70] *Life*, pp. 86-87. For a contrary opinion, Cf. Thomas Yoseloff, *A Follow of Infinite Jest* (New York, Prentice Hall, 1945), p. 84.
[71] *Tristram Shandy*, pp. 123-140.

story of the Abbess and the Novitiate, and the translation of the tenth decade of *Slawkenbergius*.

The authority of the church and the importance of the sacrament of baptism apparently are simultaneously reduced to absurdity by the comments of "Les Docteurs de Sorbonne" concerning the validity of baptism *in utero*: "That though no part of the child's body should appear, that baptism shall, nevertheless, be administered to it by injection – *par le moyen d'une petite canulle*, – *Anglice a squirt*." Tristram wonders if baptism might not be as effective if administered by injecting the father between marriage and consummation. And in the second edition of the first two volumes Sterne called attention to the fact that he had transcribed an actual document.[72]

In the curse of Bishop Ernulphus Sterne attacks what has been called the chief instrument by which the Catholic Church has carried out its authority – its power to anathematize.[73] The Curse of Bishop Ernulphus may well be in effect the anathematizing of the power of cursing. And, as in the case of the pronouncement on prenatal baptism, Sterne in the second edition showed that he had transcribed an actual document.[74]

Sterne attacks celibacy several times in *Tristram Shandy*. He handles Trim's love affair with the nun of the white hands with the tenderness that probably justified Tristram's comment: "It is enough that it contained in it the essence of all the love romances which ever have been wrote since the beginning of the world." [75] But Trim's nun was a Beguine, an order that did not take the vow of celibacy. On the other hand, the story of the Abbess and the little novitiate gave Tristram, and perhaps Sterne himself, some apprehensions.

Seeking a cure for her stiff knee, the Abbess of Andöullets journeys to Bourbon to try the hot baths. She takes along with her "a novice of the convent of about seventeen, who had been troubled by a whitlow in her middle finger, by sticking it constant-

---
[72] *Ibid.*, Work's note, p. 58.
[73] Joseph N. Gignac, "Anathema", *Catholic Encyclopedia* (New York, Catholic Encyclopedia Press, 1907), I, p. 455.
[74] *Tristram Shandy*, Work's note, p. 58, n. 3.
[75] *Tristram Shandy*, p. 575. See also p. 571 and p. 265, n. 30.

ly into the abbess's cast poultices". The journey goes happily enough until the muleteer deserts them, leaving them stranded with two mules, natural symbols of sterility. In an attempt to make the stalled animals go ahead, the novitiate persuades the abbess to utter with her the words, "bouger" and "foutre". The words are so obscene that James Aiken Work in his edition of *Tristram Shandy* has refrained from stating their true meanings. Bad as the words are, they will not make the mules go ahead, and Sterne leaves the nuns stranded.[76]

The ninth tale of the tenth decade of *Slawkenbergius* is a nearly incoherent story of a lover, who because his mistress doubts that his nose is long enough obtains an enormous one at the promontory of noses. Cross believed that Sterne while correcting the proof was still undecided about including the tale.[77]

"Learned men, brother Shandy", says Walter Shandy, "do not write dialogues on long noses for nothing". And Sterne, along with attacking 'learned blockheads", satirizes the Catholic Church for equating symbols with the objects they symbolize and for expecting the celibate orders to restrain their natural cravings. Several orders of the sisterhood were so disturbed by what the long nose symbolized that they were unable to sleep. "The nuns of St. Ursula acted the wisest – they never attempted to go to bed at all . . ." The dean of Strasbourg, the capitulars and domiciliars (capitularly assembled in the mornings to consider the case of butter'd buns) all wished they had followed the nuns of St. Ursula's example." [78] And Sterne leaves little doubt of how the nuns had been excited in his reference to "buttered buns".

In some cases better than in others, Sterne has subordinated his anti-Catholic feelings to the artistic demands of the novel. Surely few readers would want Dr. Slop left out of *Tristram Shandy*. And it might be that in his dual role of midwife and defender of authority he performs an indispenable function in the novel. David Worcester has said of the Curse of Bishop Ernulphus, "The whole excommunication, with its context, is humorous

[76] *Ibid.*, p. 510, n. 1.
[77] *Life*, p. 267.
[78] *Tristram Shandy*, p. 267.

beyond any other passage in *Tristram Shandy*." [79] And Tristram's own comment about the story of Trim's love affair with the Beguine demands assent.

But it is hard to see how the novel has been helped by the sniggering proposal of baptizing before conception. Since Sterne insists that the nose is a phallic symbol and since a false nose is not an unusual device in making laughing comedy, it is conceivable that the Tale of Slawkenbergius serves the theme of procreation and provides something laugh-at-able. But it is hard to defend the scurrilous handling of the several orders of the sisterhood. In the story of the abbess and the novitiate, the nuns and the mules are nice symbols of sterility, but not much can be said for the "hint of the impure presence" in the way the story is related.

In the case of the last story Sterne indicated that he had gone against his better judgment. Somewhere he had learned what was fitting, as the way in which *Tristram Shandy* has come to be regarded will testify. Cross has found evidence that Sterne did a great deal of revising.[80] But the revising would scarcely have been effective without Sterne's having previously acquired some principles of literary excellence. The years as a minister – the daily Bible reading, the reading of the commentaries, and the preparation of sermons – cannot be given all the credit for forming that literary judgment, but they probably did contribute to it. Sterne's writing and revising must have depended somewhat upon what Sterne believed the form of the novel should be and what purpose it was to serve. His ministry should have had a part in predetermining whether or not the novel was to make a statement, and in case it should make one, predetermined something of its nature.

There were several possibilities: *Tristram Shandy* could make a statement about itself and about the world outside. It could be so constructed that it would make none valid outside itself, or it could be a compendium of comments on the nature of things outside itself. And there was at least one more possibility: the total structure of the novel could be such that it demanded a comment

---

[79] David Worcester, *The Art of Satire* (Cambridge, Mass., Harvard University Press, 1940), p. 94.
[80] *Life*, p. 191.

from the world outside itself. Whatever kind of statement it does make depends to a certain extent upon the author's having convictions about the nature of final purposes.

Sterne's ministry should provide some clue to the author's belief about such matters. Wilbur Cross was skeptical about the concurrence of Sterne's convictions and preaching:

> He preached a sort of common-sense philosophy, which if it had little to do with Christian dogmas, never contradicted them. The evils and disorders of the world were as apparent to him as to the philosophers; yet he believed in the essential goodness of human nature and in the wise and just ways of providence. The author of Yorick's sermons, said Lady Cowper, must have been a good man; certainly a good man if he followed his instructions.[81]

A recent critic of Sterne, Lansing Van der Hammond, is inclined to agree with an endorsement of Sterne's sincerity made by Paul Stapfer in 1870:

> Sterne was short and substantial, but he possessed a virtue still more rare: I mean the sincerity of his preaching. He understood what he was saying and believed it. I don't say he practiced what he preached; that's a different matter; but he knew what he was doing and put trust in it. What the English call *cant*, and the French, *patois de Chanaan* – that unintelligible gibberish, made up of obscure biblical metaphors, badly interpreted – never came to darken either his thoughts or his delivery. There was nothing of the hypocrite in him; and however peculiar this clergyman may have been nothing could be falser than to represent him simply as a buffoon.[82]

If Hammond and Stapfer are correct, there is some reason to believe that Sterne's convictions were in agreement with the Anglican Church; Sterne's search for final purposes would have ended then where the searching of the church rested – in a theology.

As for the value of a work of art for furnishing a comment on the nature of things, Sterne the minister was committed to the belief that the Scriptures furnished the valuable commentaries. And in defending their value he, in at least one case, tended to

[81] *Life*, p. 247.
[82] *Laurence Sterne, Étude biographique et littéraire* (Paris, 1870), pp. 104-105, quoted in *Laurence Sterne's Sermons of Mr. Yorick*, p. 97.

denigrate all man-made writings. In the sermon, "Search the Scriptures", Sterne somewhat minimized the contents of the classics:

> – the natural conclusion from hence is, that in the classical authors, the expression, the sweetness of the numbers, occasioned by a musical placing of words, constitute a great part of their beauties; – whereas, in the Sacred Writings, they consist more in the greatness of the things themselves than in the words and expressions. – The ideas and expressions are so great and lofty in their own nature, that they necessarily appear magnificent in the most artless dress.[83]

What value Sterne placed on his own writing for the message it contained might well have been stated by Yorick at the end of *Tristram Shandy*: "It's a story of a COCK and a BULL, but one of best of its kind I ever heard." And it perhaps should be noticed that Yorick, the minister, said it. The change from minister into novelist, however, can be examined better in a separate chapter.

---

[83] Sermon xv. *Sterne's Works*, VII, p. 230.

IV

THE TRANSITION FROM MINISTER TO NOVELIST

In the present chapter the author's initial separation of himself from the work will be considered. In the three previous ones it has been contended that although *Tristram Shandy* was a work of fiction, the life and ministry of Laurence Sterne had been responsible for a great deal of the way it was written. Now, the reasons for Sterne's separating himself from *Tristram Shandy* will be presented, and the first installment of the novel will be offered as evidence of the author's effort to keep himself and his work apart.

In the first place, the minister's divergent attitudes toward sacred and profane writings will be noticed, and inferences will be drawn about the minister's reasons for separating himself from the latter. Next, the likelihood will be considered of Sterne's examining the "standard" novel of the 1860's but following the precepts and practices of older writers. It will be noticed particularly that Sterne could have, and probably did, learn from such writers as Rabelais, Cervantes, and Swift the valuable lesson of keeping his work at some distance from himself. Brief notice will then be taken of the anonymous fashion in which *Tristram Shandy* was presented to the public and of its being read without the readers' guessing that the author was a clergyman. Finally, the conclusion will be advanced that Sterne not only learned from the earlier writers but added a refinement of his own. In some detail the composite figure of Parson Yorick will be considered as the agency by which the minister author ensured his distinctness from the *persona* and his participation in the story.

It would be surprising if a man who had spent twenty years in the ministry before entering upon a book like *Tristram Shandy* had not reached certain conclusions concerning sacred and profane writings, nor is it unlikely that such convictions might have made him feel uneasy, even until the time he had written all but the last volume of *Tristram Shandy*. It is not improbable that a sense of guilt lay behind the metaphor in the letter written to Thomas Hazelridge shortly after the seventh and eighth volumes of *Tristram Shandy* had been published:

Have you seen my 7 & 8 graceless Children – but I am doing penance for them in begetting a couple of ecclesiastical ones – which are to stand penance (again) in sheets about the middle of Septr – they will appear in the 3d and 4 Vols of Yorick.[1]

It would seem strange for Sterne not to have felt that in his secular profession he had been, as Augustine had said of the artist, "a maker of lies",[2] or that to a certain extent he had been "dallying with the devil", as Coleridge was later to remark about Sterne's writings.[3]

As a minister, Sterne had preached and based his reason for preaching on the "awful sacred pages" of the Old and New Testaments. He had not quibbled about the matter of inspiration. The Gospel was God's authoritative message to mankind, and it had been recorded by those divinely inspired. In the same discourse in which he called the writers "Divine Penmen", he spoke warmly of the "ten thousand sublime and noble passages, which by the rules of sound criticism and reason, may be demonstrated to be truly elegant and beautiful". And he denounced whoever would find less than perfection in the Scriptures:

Presumptious man: – Shall he, who is but dust and ashes, dare to find fault with the words of that Being, who first inspired man with language, and taught his mouth to utter.[4]

There is evidence that Sterne even regretted the necessity for a minister's using fictitious examples in explaining the Scripture.

---

[1] *Letters*, p. 76.
[2] "Soliloquia" II, X *Confessions* III, VI, p. 126.
[3] *Coleridge's Miscellaneous Criticism*, p. 12.
[4] *Sermons* II, in *Sterne's Works*, VII, p. 231 f.; Cf. *Sermons* I, in VI, p. 112, for identical phrasing.

Although Sterne contended that the Scriptures had been written "with that force and majesty with which never man wrote" and that they had been "conveyed with clearness and perspicuity to mankind", he nevertheless admitted that a minister was needed to make the divinely inspired words understood.[5] The fault was not in the words, but in the nature of the reader or hearer. In commenting on the text, "For none of us liveth to himself", he says as much:

There is not a sentence in scripture, which strikes a soul with greater astonishment; – and one might as easily engage to clear up the darkest problem in geometry to an ignorant mind, as make a sordid one comprehend the truth and reasonableness of this plain proposition.[6]

In another sermon he says that since self-love stands in the way of understanding, one must sometimes stoop in order to effect understanding: "Those who have sought the reformation of mankind ... have endeavoured by stratagem to get beyond it, and by a skillful address to deceive it."[7] A further disparagement of the means can be seen in the beginning of the sermon, "The Prodigal Son".

I know not whether the remark is to our honour or otherwise, that lessons of wisdom have never such power over us, as when they are wrought into the heart, through the groundwork of a story which engages the passions: Is it that we are like iron, and must be heated before we can be wrought upon? or, is the heart so in love with deceit, that where a true report will not reach it, we must cheat it with a fable, to come at truth?[8]

Of Sterne's curiosity concerning the nature of language, sacred or profane, direct evidence is lacking. But that he was curious about

---

[5] That Sterne thought of the minister as one who delivers the Gospel of its meaning is suggested by the extensive use of the midwife theme in the beginning of *Tristram Shandy*. Parson Yorick's good horses are ridden to death to fetch a midwife for the members of the congregation. He rides a sorry jade until he pays the license fee for an old woman in the parish who will later attempt to deliver Tristram. After the licensing, Yorick goes well mounted again; but this change is one in a series of events that lead to the death of Yorick.
[6] *Sermons* I, VI, p. 81.
[7] *Ibid.*, I, VI, p. 40.
[8] *Ibid.*, I, VI, p. 227.

it, especially in view of his ministerial and literary careers, can scarcely be doubted. If it could be assumed that Sterne began with the Gospel of John –

In the beginning was the Word, and the Word was with God, and the Word was God. The same was in the beginning with God. All things were made by him; and without him nothing was made that was made –

and that he followed the study of the "Logos" through the polemics of the Fathers, the sermons of the Anglican Divines, and the various commentaries on the Scriptures, one could be sure that Sterne had early become aware that there were other theories of creation and of the creating power of words besides that of the Judaeo-Christian religion.

Indications of Sterne's familiarity with other systems of thought concerning language and its creating power can be found outside of his sermons. Sterne had known Bishop Warburton's *Divine Legation of Moses*, a comparative study of Judaism and Christianity with other religions, in which language was treated as an important aspect of religion.[9] The catalogue of Sterne's books lists several works which deal with such matters. And Sterne refers to several works of the same nature in *Tristram Shandy*. Moreover, there is in *Tristram Shandy* the ridicule of Walter Shandy's concern with the power of names, especially with that of Trismegistus.

Although the years in the ministry might well have been primarily responsible for the author's keeping the narrator and the book separate from Sterne the minister, the authorial posture was in accordance with nearly traditional practice. And, according to Maynard Mack, "an assumed identity, a *persona*, a mask, was a specialty in the Augustan Age".[10] Many of the writers with whom Sterne was familiar had found ways to disengage themselves from

---

[9] For example, Warburton says: "The religion of names, as we have shown, was a matter of great consequence in Egypt. It was one of their essential Superstitions; it was one of their native Inventions; and the first of them that they communicated to the Greeks." 2d ed. (London, Printed for the Executor of the late Mr. Giles Fletcher, 1742), p. 286.

[10] *The Augustans*, ed. Maynard Mack, in *English Masterpieces* (New York, Prentice Hall, 1950), p. 12.

their products, and from their first-person narrators (if they made use of such). And in certain cases the writers had explicitly stated that they avoided dealing with sacred matters in their secular works. Although there was a variety of sources from which Sterne could have found examples of authors who had separated themselves from their works, only those with whom there is good reason to believe he had commerce will be considered.

But, before they are taken up, the attention Sterne gave to three contemporaries – Fielding, Johnson, and Voltaire – must be looked at. Although the practice of "separation" was well-nigh traditional among writers in several genres, some of the major novelists of Sterne's day had deviated from the practice. And according to H. K. Russell the author of *Tristram Shandy* examined the "standard" novel in order to write a better one:

> There is reason to believe that Sterne, more than has been realized, consciously examined the "standard" novel as represented by Fielding's work, critically (not merely whimsically), indicated its shortcomings, and demonstrated what seemed to him preferable techniques.[11]

That Sterne's major improvement over Fielding's *Tom Jones* was in the use of the "invisible novelist", a refinement of the novel, which in the twentieth century was to become standard practice, has been pointed out by Bernard De Voto.[12]

Sterne must have given some attention to Johnson's *Rasselas* and Voltaire's *Candide*, which were published in the same year he began writing *Tristram Shandy*.[13] He asked his prospective printer to issue *Tristram Shandy* "in two small volumes of the size of *Rasselas*, and on the same paper and type".[14] And early in

---

[11] "*Tristram Shandy* and the Techniques of the Novel", *SP*, XLII (1945), p. 581.
[12] *The World of Fiction* (Boston, Houghton Mifflin Company, 1950), pp. 200 f.
[13] Samuel Johnson, *The Prince of Abyssinia. A Tale*, 2 vols. (London, R. and J. Dodsley, 1759). François Marie Arouet de Voltaire, *Candide, Or, All for the Best* (London, J. Nourse, 1759). See Andrew Block, *English Novel, 1740-1850* (London, Dawsons of Pall Mall, 1961), I, pp. 124, 246.
[14] *Letters*, p. 81, n. 2. See also Curtis's "The First Printer of *Tristram Shandy*", *PMLA*, XLVIII (1932), pp. 777-789.

the novel he appealed to the "Bright Goddess" of inspiration to take Tristram under her protection if she were not too busy with the affairs of Candide.[15]

According to Irma Shirwood, the chief fault in *Tom Jones* and in *Rasselas* is that "the author keeps intruding himself between the reader and the imaginative world of the novel".[16] The practice was due, she argues, to the authors' regarding themselves "not only as tellers of tales but as critics and philosophers, preachers and reformers".[17] Although she does not mention Voltaire, his purpose in *Candide* does not appear to have differed from that of his English contemporaries.

Whatever use Sterne might have made of *Tom Jones, Rasselas,* or *Candide* – works which did not employ the first-person narrative as *Tristram Shandy* did, he has been traditionally associated with those of Rabelais, Montaigne, Cervantes, Burton, and Swift. Although they represent different literary types and different methods of presentation were employed in them, each has been credited with exercising some influence upon Sterne.

When Sterne began writing his novel, it would not have been unusual for him to turn to Swift, whose sermons he had borrowed from in preparing at least two of his own.[18] Before *Tristram Shandy* had been published, Sterne wrote that Swift kept a due distance from Rabelais, and that he was keeping a due distance from Swift.[19] Sterne could scarcely have failed to notice that the author had kept himself apart from the work by presenting the *Travels into several Remote Nations of the World* as being written "by Lemuel Gulliver, first a surgeon and then a captain on several Ships".[20] Whatever edition Sterne read would have made

---

[15] *Tristram Shandy*, p. 17. See also C. J. Rawlinson, "*Tristram Shandy* and *Candide*", *N&Q*, CCM (1958), p. 226.
[16] "The Novelists as Commentators", in *The Age of Johnson: Essays Presented to Chauncey Brewster Tinker* (New Haven, Yale University Press, 1949), p. 124.
[17] *Ibid.*, p. 117.
[18] *Sermons of Mr. Yorick*, p. 83, n. 4, pp. 151, 152.
[19] *Letters*, p. 76.
[20] Jonathan Swift, *Gulliver's Travels*, ed. Herbert Davis, with an Introduction by Harold Williams (Oxford, Basil Blackwell, 1959), p. 2.

little difference: until the Faulkner edition of Swift's works in 1735, Swift's name had been omitted from the title page of the *Travels*. The identification had then been offset by the inclusion of the letters of Gulliver, and of Sympson to whom the publication had allegedly been intrusted.[21]

According to Maynard Mack, "Swift's irony always presupposes a fictitious writer". And he further states that it is a "fatal error" to identify Swift with his *persona*, Gulliver.[22] Bullitt sees a practical reason for Swift's concealing himself behind different identities in the political pamphlets. "The penalties for sedition were severe, and Swift's pamphlets were more than once condemned as both libelous and seditious." He concludes, however, that in Swift's writing, taken as a whole, more than personal safety was involved: "The more fundamental reason was that Swift could conceal behind ironic masks the intenisty of his personal involvement." [23]

Tradition has credited Rabelais with exerting an even greater influence on Sterne than Swift.[24] Although the writer of *Gargantua* and *Pantagruel* used a third person narrative, he, like Swift and Sterne, was a churchman and a writer. Rabelais had at the beginning of *Pantagruel* disclaimed the writing as being his own, by saying that it had been found by the chance opening of "a great brazen tomb", and that

[21] *Ibid.*, pp. xxii-xxvi, 2, 297, 299.
[22] *The Augustans* in *English Masterpieces*, pp. 12, 16. See also the statement by Ricardo Quinatana, "Situational Satire: A Commentary on the Method of Swift", *University of Toronto Quarterly*, XVII (1948), pp. 130-136. To do so is "to obscure the artist, the craftsman...."
[23] John M. Bullitt, *Jonathan Swift and the Anatomy of Satire* (Cambridge, Harvard University Press, 1953), p. 56 f. Apparently, the question of Swift's adopting a mask for reasons of religious convictions has never been raised.
[24] *Life*, p. 140. Long before Cross, John Ferriar had pointed out Sterne's obligations to Rabelais. Cf. *Illustrations of Sterne*, 1, 140; see also Work's numerous notations concerning the allusions to *Gargantua* and *Pantagruel* in the Odyssey Press edition of *Tristram Shandy*, pp. 191, n. 2, 194, n. 4, 200, n. 13, 219, n. 1, 226, n. 3, 234, n. 10, 235, n. 12, 240, n. 22, 264, n. 2, 383, n. 1, 387, n. 2, and 632, n. 2; see also Lewis Perry Curtis's notes calling attention to mention of Rabelais in *Letters*, pp. 59, n. 1, 77, n. 1, and 114, n. 2. One can also find references to Rabelais in *Letters*, pp. 76, 79, and 132.

I Rabelais, though unworthy, was sent for thither, and with much help of those spectacles, whereby the art of reading dim writings, and letters that do not appear to the sight is practised as Aristotle teaches it; did translate the book.[25]

Whatever reason he might have had for posing as a translator, Rabelais had made it clear that he intended to avoid profanation. He wrote: "The antiquity and genealogy of Gargantua has been reserved for our use, more full than that of any other except the Messias, whereof I mean not to speak; for it belongs not unto my province." [26]

Cervantes, like Rabelais, used the third-person narrative point of view. He, moreover, represents a further remove from the Reverend Mr. Sterne and his narrator, Tristram, in that he was not a churchman. He has long been credited with exercising an influence comparable with that of Rabelais. And the novel and the letters contain numerous signs of Sterne's familiarity with him.[27] Sterne showed a preference for him by vowing in the third volume of *Tristram Shandy*: "By the ashes of my dear Rabelais, and dearer Cervantes." [28] Cross states that although Sterne's inspiration came chiefly from Rabelais, "the presence of Cervantes is felt in one place or another in every volume of *Tristram Shandy*".[29]

A greater degree of separation between author and novel appeared in *Don Quixote* than in *Gargantua* and *Pantagruel*. Rabelais had posed as the translator of the writings on the bronze tablets; Cervantes, as the recorder of the translation made for him of the writings of Cid Hamet Benengeli. What is more important, Cervantes used the separation to exculpate himself for artistic ineptitude or religious turpitude in writing *Don Quixote*: "If any point in it falls short of your expectations, I am of the Opinion 'twas more the fault of the Infidel author." [30]

---

[25] François Rabelais, *Gangantua and Pantagruel* (New York, Dodd, Mead & Co., n.d.), pp. 8-9.
[26] *Ibid.*, p. 10.
[27] *Letters*, p. 18, n. 4, 5; pp. 50, 178, n. 5; pp. 191, 338, 529, n. 1; p. 628.
[28] *Tristram Shandy*, p. 191.
[29] *Life*, p. 140.
[30] Ozell's Revision of the Translation of Peter Motteux, *Don Quixote by*

Although Cervantes was not a cleric, "he was a good Catholic", says an authority on *Don Quixote*, Americo Castro, who has found that the rough drafts of the work contain "numerous emendations of Ecclesiastical and moral character". He also points out that "Don Quixote says in his discourse upon Arms and Letters that he does not speak 'of divine letters, the aim of which is to raise the soul to Heaven, for with an end so infinite no other can be compared' (1 : 37)." [31]

Since Castro next speaks of the likeness in this respect of Cervantes to Montaigne, it is convenient to look briefly at the author of the *Essais*, of whom Sterne himself wrote that he had conned as much as his prayer book.[32] James Aiken Work has credited him with having exerted an even greater influence on Sterne than Rabelais did.[33] Montaigne is a step further away from Sterne than Cervantes is, for his work was not a novel and it was a most personal kind of writing; but he did make an explicit statement about the necessity of keeping secular writings apart from ecclesiastical matters. Castro says of Cervantes' likeness to Montaigne: "Here perhaps without Cervantes even intending it, he coincides with Montaigne, who is solely interested in human affairs within the scope of human experience." He, then, quotes Montaigne:

La doctrine divine tient mieux rang *à part* comme reine et dominatrice.... Les raisons divines se considèrent plus vénérablement et en leur style qu'appariées aux discours humains.[34] (*Essais*, I, 56.)

Robert Burton, another of the writers with whom Sterne is believed to have been very familiar, although his work was a straight treatise, was closer to Sterne than Montaigne in that he was a churchman and writer. Since the publication of Dr. John Ferriar's *Illustrations of Sterne* in 1798, there has been little doubt about

---

Miguel de Cervantes, Modern Library (New York, Random House, 1930), p. xix, p. 51.
[31] In, Edwin B. Knowles, "Cervantes and English Literature", in *Cervantes across the Centuries*, eds. Angel Flores and Bernadette (New York, Dryden Press, 1947), p. 284.
[32] *Ibid.*
[33] *Tristram Shandy*, p. 191, n. 2.
[34] Knowles, p. 284.

Sterne's indebtedness to Burton's *Anatomy of Melancholy*.[35] Ferriar argued that Sterne took from the *Anatomy of Melancholy* not only a great deal of content but also a certain amount of method. Burton presented Democritus, Jr. as the author of the work, but in the beginning of the section entitled "Democritus, to the Reader", he (Burton) declared that he "would not willingly be known". Near the end of the section, and after he had described the character and the appropriateness of the *persona* – and here one can see how Burton's and Sterne's cases were alike – Burton explained why he wished to remain anonymous.

If I have overshot myself in this which hath hitherto been said, or that it is, which I am sure some will object, too fantastical, too light and comical for a Divine, too satirical for one of my profession, I will presume to answer with Erasmus, in like case, 'tis not I, but Democritus, Democritus *dixit*.[36]

There is good reason to believe that Sterne was indebted to Rabelais, Montaigne, Cervantes, Burton, and Swift for the *persona*. The first installment of *Tristram Shandy*, in 1760, showed signs that Sterne had avoided calling attention to his "band or hassock". There was something like a public proclamation in the title, "The Life and opinions of Tristram Shandy, Gentleman", that the work contained the life and opinions of someone other than that of Laurence Sterne, Prebendary of York. The epigraph, "It is not actions, but opinions concerning actions, which disturb men", suggested that the disturbing opinions were those of Tristram Shandy. According to Hammond, "none of the reviewers knew that Sterne was a clergyman when they penned their favorable reviews during the first two months of 1760. Had they known this fact . . . they would have been much more harsh toward the production." [37]

The work began in a fashion consonant with the title. Tristram, the narrator, related an event in his make-believe life that a

---

[35] Alan B. Howes, *Yorick and the Critics* (New Haven, Yale University Press, 1958), p. 88.
[36] Robert Burton, *Anatomy of Melancholy*, American Reprint of Last London ed. (Philadelphia, J. W. Moore, 1852), p. 76.
[37] Howes, p. 5.

minister would scarcely have discussed in public, and in accents as foreign to the minister as the choice of a subject was. And, as if the indications were not enough to separate the narrator from the minister writer, Yorick, a minister that had been fashioned to resemble the author, was included in the narrative. The character was introduced, as early as the seventh chapter, as the licenser of the midwife who was to be present at Tristram's birth; but he was subsequently presented with more detail than such a function in the novel would seem to warrant. And after he had been presented, he was removed with a great deal of finality: The narrator only related the cause of Yorick's death, showed his epitaph, and transcribed the accents with which it was read, but also separated the account of Yorick from the subsequent material by inserting two black pages between them.

Before taking up in more detail the presentation of Yorick, one must add that although Sterne probably had learned from Swift and others the value of using a *persona*, his new profession made demands of its own, and, particularly, the kind of novel Sterne began writing militated against his presenting himself as the writer. Percy Lubbock must have had *Tristram Shandy* in mind when he concluded the following account of autobiography:

Autobiography – it is a regular literary form, and yet it is one which refuses the recognized principles of literary form; its natural right is to *seem* [italics mine] wayward and inconsequent; its charm is in the fidelity with which it follows the winding course of the writer's thought as he muses upon the past, and the writer is not expected to guide in an orderly design, but to let it wander free. Formlessness becomes actually the mark of right form in literature of this class; and a novel presented as fictitious autobiography gets the same advantage.[38]

Even though Sterne's prior considerations for separating himself from *Tristram Shandy* should be disregarded, the fact that he chose to write a fictitious autobiography made it categorically imperative that the separation be made. Whatever reasons he might have had for writing a biography of Tristram Shandy, once

---

[38] *The Craft of Fiction* (New York, Charles Scribner's Sons, n.d.), pp. 131 f.

having made the decision, he must have seen the advantages of autobiography over biography. Hartley in this connection quotes Dr. Johnson's remark that " 'no man is as fit to be a man's biographer as the man himself' ".[39] And Sterne's artistic sense must have counselled him that the more the fictive autobiographer looked like Laurence Sterne, the less would be the appearance of objective reality. There is, of course, no direct evidence that Sterne reasoned about why he should separate himself from Tristram or from the novel, although it does seem likely that he did so.

But there is within the novel an agency by which Sterne ensures both his distinctness from and participation in his story, the character of Yorick. It is not suggested that at the beginning Yorick was a replica of Sterne but that at the beginning he was much closer to Sterne than Tristram Shandy was. Though by the end of the novel Sterne had developed a Yorick who participated in the affairs of the Shandy family and who in the next novel became the hero and first-person narrator, in the beginning of *Tristram Shandy*, Yorick was introduced as one who had played a small part in helping to get the narrator, Tristram, born. And after he had been described at some length as a goodhearted, jesting minister, whose merriment led to disaster, he was removed from the scene.

If the presentation of Yorick can be accepted as serving to set the novel apart from the author for the benefit of Sterne, the minister, to set the author apart from the novel for the benefit of Tristram, the *persona*, and to permit the author to have it both ways – be both *in* and *out* of the story – not only will the contention that *Tristram Shandy* is primarily a work of fiction instead of Sterne's autobiography be better established, but the artistry displayed by the author in a hitherto neglected aspect of his novel can be better appreciated.

First of all, Yorick's peculiar nature was necessary in order for him to serve the author in the way we have indicated. He must resemble Sterne, but not be a replica of him; he must be a fictional

---

[39] *This Is Lorence* (Chapel Hill, University of North Carolina Press, 1943), p. ix.

character, but not the entirely fictitious one James Aiken Work would have him be:

Parson Yorick is, of course, a sublimated, idealized Sterne – Sterne as he wished himself known to the world; but however effective as a bit of special pleading for the author, he is too self-consciously drawn for perfect credibility as a character.[40]

Work, by calling Yorick "a sublimated, idealized Sterne", followed the example of Cross.[41] According to a student of Sterne's sermons, "it has long been recognized that in the character of Parson Yorick, which emerges from the pages of *Tristram Shandy*, Sterne was drawing a picture of himself as Vicar of Sutton".[42] However, so long as Tristram was believed to be Sterne, it would have been difficult to identify Yorick with Sterne. Howes has said of the confusion: "Yorick, Tristram, and Laurence Sterne became hopelessly entangled in the public mind." [43] Now, that Tristram is less closely identified with the author, Yorick's resemblance to Sterne has received more attention. In some cases Yorick has been regarded as a portrait of Sterne. Cross and Work are more nearly correct in calling him "a sublimated, idealized Sterne", although Work has not taken into account the fact that Yorick was a variant of Shakespeare's jester as well as a sublimated, idealized Prebendary of York.

"Yorick the Parson", says B. H. Lehman, "was descended from the greatest and purest jester of them all, who having no lines to say, exists as the absolute jester of the imagination".[44] A study of the presentation of Yorick in *Tristram Shandy* will reveal that Sterne's character is not only something of the jester in *Hamlet* but also something in his own right and something of Sterne himself.

Evidence that the Yorick in *Tristram Shandy* is a permutation of the Yorick of *Hamlet* can be seen by comparing the more ob-

---

[40] *Tristram Shandy*, p. lxviii.
[41] *Life*, p. 62.
[42] Lansing Van der Hammond, *Laurence Sterne's Sermons of Mr. Yorick* (New Haven, Yale University Press, 1948), p. 17.
[43] Howes, p. 5.
[44] B. H. Lehman, "Of Time, Personality and the Author", *University of California Publications in English*, VII (1941), p. 238.

vious features of the jester in *Hamlet* and in *Tristram Shandy*. In *Hamlet* the existence of Yorick is posited by no more than a skull and the way Hamlet and the gravedigger remember him. The skull is identified by the gravedigger, who remembers and hates the jester for having made him the butt of a jest. After the skull has been identified, Hamlet remembers Yorick with love and admiration for his many acts of kindness and his exceptional qualities as a jester.

Sterne's Yorick, like the original, exists at first only in the mind of a fictional character, Tristram. Hamlet's gravedigger knocked the skull "about the sconce with a dirty shovel" after he had unearthed it and expended his resentment in a futile manner for his long-remembered humiliation. Sterne's "grave ones", especially those who affected gravity, whom Parson Yorick has offended, take immediate action against the one who has made them the butt of his jokes, by delivering blows that cause his death. Sterne's Yorick says as much:

I beseech thee to take a view of my head. I see nothing that ails it, replied *Eugenius*. Then, alas! my friend, said *Yorick*, let me tell you, that 'tis so bruised and mis-shapen'd with the blows which ***** and *****, and some others have so handsomely given me in the dark.... Yorick's last breath was hanging upon his trembling lips ready to depart as he uttered this.[45]

Up to a certain point, aspects of the original are particularized in the copy. The first Yorick was remembered by Hamlet with love and admiration for his infinite jests and "most excellent fancy". The second is presented as "not an unkind-hearted man", who "had never the heart to refuse the loan" of his horse to anyone.[46] Instead of "a most excellent fancy", he has enough keenness of perception to see through the pretensions of those in power but he lacks enough prudence to pretend that he has not observed them.[47] The infinite capacity for jesting of the first becomes particularized in the second: "His character was, – he loved a jest in his heart – and as he saw himself in the true point of ridicule,

---

[45] *Tristram Shandy*, p. 31.
[46] *Ibid.*, p. 21.
[47] *Ibid.*, p. 27.

THE TRANSITION FROM MINISTER TO NOVELIST 93

he would say, he could not be angry with others for seeing him in a light, in which he so strongly saw himself." [48]

Sterne's Yorick is then developed with certain characteristics of his own, but Eugenius, the friend of the jesting parson, recognizes "the lack of spleen or malevolent intent" [49] behind the jests. Eugenius also knows that which his friend never discovers until it is too late: the jesting will lead to disaster. And Eugenius vainly tries to explain the situation to Sterne's Yorick:

> I cannot suspect it in a man whom I esteem, that there is the least spur or malevolence of intent in these sallies. – I believes and know them to be truly honest and sportive: – But consider, my dear lad, that fools cannot distinguish this, – and knaves will not; and thou knowest for what it is, either to provoke the one, or to make merry with the other. – whenever they associate for mutual defense, depend upon it, they will carry on the war in such a manner against thee, my dear friend, as to make thee heartily sick of it, and of thy life too.[50]

A still further remove from the original can be observed in the highly complicated causes of the death of the second. Despite the warnings of Eugenius, Yorick believes "that as not one of his jests had been made through any malignancy; – but on the contrary, from an honesty of mind, and a mere jocundity of humour, they would all of them be crossed out in due course". He is finally forced to realize what his friend had known all along, and the recognition is a contributing cause of his death.

> *Yorick*, however, fought it out with all imaginable gallantry for some time; till over-power'd by numbers, and worn out at length by the calamities of war, – but more so, by the ungenerous manner in which it was carried on, – he threw down the sword; and though he kept up his appearance to the last, he died, nevertheless, as was generally thought, quite broken hearted.[51]

"What inclined Eugenius to the same opinion" is Yorick's deathbed confession: "I might say with Sancho Panza, that should I recover, and 'Mitres thereupon be suffer'd to rain down from Heaven as hail, not one of 'em would fit." It is possible to see in

---

[48] *Ibid.*, p. 19.
[49] *Ibid.*, p. 29.
[50] *Ibid.*, p. 28.
[51] *Ibid.*, p. 30.

Yorick's last words a sense of unworthiness, a condition that has recently come about.

Further removes from the original can be observed in Sterne's portrait of Yorick: The motives behind his actions are no better understood by others than are the intentions behind his jests. He is credited with having said and done more than he actually had. And he is either unable or unwilling to explain his motives and intentions. Whenever Parson Yorick castigates folly, his parishioners believe that he does so because of malevolence, not from a sense of duty. Whenever he tries to provide for the welfare of his flock, the worst is believed of him, and he says nothing in defense of his actions. Finding that the expense of furnishing good horses to "fetch the midwife" left "nothing for the many comfortless scenes he was compelled to visit", Yorick's solution was to ride a "poor devil of a horse" that no one else would want to ride. It was then believed that his ridiculous nature caused him to ride the "lean, sorry, jackass of a horse". Instead of explaining, he "chose rather to join in the laugh against himself".

After Yorick has paid the license fee for a midwife for the parish and he can ride a good horse once more, his parishioners now believe that he rode the sorry nags to save money for himself.

In the second installment of *Tristram Shandy* Yorick's kinship to the original is noticed, and Yorick's exorbitant reputation, proneness for being misunderstood, and unwillingness to explain his actions are reviewed.

Yorick, no doubt, as Shakespeare said of his ancestor – "*was a man of jest*", but it was temper'd with something which withheld him from ... many ungracious pranks, of which he undeservedly bore the blame; – but it was his misfortune all his life long to bear the imputation of saying and doing a thousand things of which (unless my esteem blinds me) his nature was incapable. All I blame him for – or rather, all I blame and alternately like him for, was that singularity of his temper, which would never suffer him to take pains to set a story right with the world, however in his power. In every ill usage of that sort, be acted as in the affair of his lean horse – he could have explained it to his honour, but his spirit was above it.[52]

---

[52] *Ibid.*, p. 324.

The final misunderstanding of Sterne's Yorick is that after he has died he becomes confused with the original. Eugenius, "by leave of Yorick's executors, laid a plain marble slab upon the grave, with no more than these three words of inscription serving both for his epitaph and elegy".

["Alas poor Yorick".]
Ten times in a day has Yorick's ghost the consolation to hear this monumental inscription read over with such a variety of plaintive tones, as denote a general pity and esteem for him; – a foot-way crossing the church-yard close by the side of his grave, – not a passenger goes by without stopping to cast a look upon it, and sighing as he wolks on,
Alas, poor Yorick! [53]

In the *Sentimental Journey Through France and Italy* when Yorick is issued a passport because he has been confused with Shakespeare's jester, he has difficulty in explaining who he is.

Had it been for anyone but the king's jester, added the Count, I could not have it these two hours. – Mons. le Count, said I. I am not the king's court jester. – But you are Yorick? Yes. – *Et vous plaisantez?* Indeed I did jest – but was not paid for it – 'twas entirely at my own expense.... We have no jester at Court ... there is nothing for a jester to make a jest. *Voila un persiflage!* cried the Count.[54]

In *Tristram Shandy*, Tristram disingenuously accounts for the likeness and the difference between the two Yoricks. After he has introduced the parson of the parish who had paid the license fee for the midwife, he begins a chapter with the words: "Yorick was the parson's name." He then proceeds to establish a connection between his clergyman and a Danish ancestor. By studying the records of the Yorick family, he learns that "in the reign of Horwendillus, king of Denmark, in whose court it seems an ancestor of this Mr. Yorick's, and from whom he was lineally descended, held a considerable post to the day of his death".

Tristram next conjectures that a connection exists between his jester and Shakespeare's.

---

[53] *Ibid.*, p. 32.
[54] *A Sentimental Journey Through France and Italy*, World Classics ed. (London, Oxford University Press, 1948), p. 161.

It has often come to my head, that this post could be no other than that of the king's chief jester; and that *Hamlet's Yorick* in our *Shakespeare*, many of whose plays, you know, are founded upon authenticated facts, was certainly the very man.[55]

But after Tristram has established a tentative reason for the likeness between the two Yoricks, he finds another for the difference: "in nine hundred years", the English climate might have made some changes in the Yorick family, or the Danish blood "might all have run out". Still, a trace of the Danish ancestor remains in the remote descendant, for he "scatters his gibes and his jests about him". And when he is dying, "Eugenius could perceive [that] a stream of lambent fire lighted up for a moment in his eyes; – faint picture of those flashes of his spirit, which (as *Shakespeare* said of his ancestor) were wont to set the table in a roar!"

The jester in *Tristram Shandy* is much more the product of Sterne's creating than of Sterne's copying. To serve as an agency by which Sterne could ensure both his distinctness from and participation in the story, Yorick must be enough like Sterne the minister for the resemblance to be easily noticed, far more than by the fact that both are parsons. According to Work, he was "too self-consciously drawn for perfect credibility as a fictional character". Sterne's chief biographer, Cross, although he believed that Tristram was like the author,[56] admits that "as many times related, Sterne depicted himself as prebendary and rural parson in the indiscreet and outspoken Yorick, who scattered his gibes and his jests about him, never thinking they could be used against him. Other characteristics of Sterne came out in Mr. Tristram Shandy." [57] A recent biographer, Willard Connelly, in *Laurence Sterne as Yorick*, has declared that "not as the infant Tristram but as a country parson, Yorick Sterne on an early page inserted himself ... Yorick was drawn from life." [58]

It had generally been agreed upon by the biographers that

---

[55] *Tristram Shandy*, p. 124.
[56] *Tristram Shandy*, lviii.
[57] *Life*, p. 200.
[58] London, The Bodley Head, 1958, p. 21.

Yorick can be recognized as the author. The Reverend Mr. Sterne also had offended certain "grave ones", church politicians (especially his uncle and patron), who could and did retaliate by putting an end to his hopes for ecclesiastical preferment. Although it is doubtful that the motives of the author had been as guileless as those of his well-meaning Parson Yorick, it is fairly certain that in other respects the resemblance was close enough for Sterne to identify himself with him, to expect the reader to recognize the identity, and to emphasize the difference between himself and the hero of the novel, Tristram.

Perhaps Yorick is an idealized Sterne; certainly, he is a character in *Tristram Shandy*. And as Yorick the Parson, he is a combination of the fictional and the real. He is Sterne's Yorick, derived from the jester in *Hamlet*: he is a sublimated, idealized parson (according to Cross and Work), who has been derived from Sterne himself. As such, he could take his place in the novel and function in the way it has been indicated.

Although several writers have pointed out the important fact that Yorick is recognizably like Sterne the minister, little notice has been taken of the almost complete difference Sterne made between the minister who was Yorick and the writer who is Tristram. Even less notice has been taken, and probably because of the fact that it had not been made very noticeable, that although the difference between Yorick and Tristram is nearly complete, there are, in the presentation of Yorick, a few indications that the man who was once a minister has some connection with Tristram and with the writing of *Tristram Shandy*. These almost obscure hints deserve some consideration for what they suggest concerning the author's view of the practical advantages of the second profession over the first and of how *Tristram Shandy* came to be written.

First of all, Yorick the minister could not or would not say anything in defense of himself. The ministerial career had not otherwise permitted Yorick to do justice to himself. Nothing appears concerning Yorick's preaching, but comments are made and pertinent examples are given of the good minister's failures to make himself known by either deeds or words as a good minister.

According to one of the comments, Yorick was troubled by the way his actions were misunderstood:

What were his views in this, and in every other action of his life, – or rather what were the opinions which floated in the brains of other people concerning it, was a thought which too much floated in his own, and too often broke in upon his rest when he should have been sound asleep.[59]

On the same page Tristram states the hopelessness of Yorick's making a good impression by anything he did:

There is a fatality attends the actions of some men: order them as they will, they pass through a certain medium which so distorts them from their true directions – that with all the titles to praise which a rectitude of heart can give, the doors of them are nevertheless forced to live and die without them.[60]

Yorick's actions are unfavorably interpreted in the case of the midwife: when Yorick lends his good horses to fetch the midwife, his generosity is not appreciated but abused. When he rides a poor horse to save something for charity, his humble appearance excites derision. And when he pays the license fee for a midwife in the parish and goes well-mounted again, he is no longer rediculed but he is now condemned for his avarice.

Yorick's words are no better understood than the deeds. By honestly calling whoever committed a dirty action, "a dirty fellow", and by laughing at those who affected gravity "as a cloak for ignorance or folly", he was regarded as malevolent, and decisive action was taken against him.

The difference between Yorick's position and Tristram's is demonstrated instead of stated: Yorick could have explained his actions and his words "to his honour, but his spirit was above it". It is obvious that Tristram not only is unhampered by any such reticence but is able to explain the motives of Yorick "to his honour".

The explicit statement of Yorick's connection with Tristram and the autobiography Tristram is writing is that Yorick paid the

[59] *Tristram Shandy*, p. 23.
[60] *Ibid.*

THE TRANSITION FROM MINISTER TO NOVELIST 99

license fee for the midwife who was present at Tristram's birth. There is, however, a curiously detailed description of the midwife's license:

> He cheerfully paid the fees for the ordinary's licence himself ... so that betwixt them both, the good woman was fully invested in the real and corporal possession of her office, together with all its *rights, members, and appurtenances, whatsoever.*
>
> These last words, you must know, were not according to the old form in which such licenses, faculties and powers usually ran, which in like cases had heretofore been granted to the sisterhood. But it was according to a neat *Formula* of *Didius* his own devising, who having a particular turn for taking to pieces and new framing all over again, all kinds of instruments in that way....[61]

James Aiken Work has not only noticed but has called attention to it as "a satirical representation of Dr. Francis Topham, an able Yorkshire lawyer ... who had been the object of Sterne's ridicule in the 'Political Romance', also entitled the 'history of a Good Warm Watchcoat'." [62] Work, furthermore, and in agreement with Cross, says that the writing career began with that attempt:

> "Till he had finished his Watchcoat", it was said he hardly knew that he could write at all, much less with humour, "so as to make his readers laugh". Now encouraged by the success of this *jeu d'esprit*, in which his later satirical technique and the hobby horses of my father and my uncle Toby were prefigures, Sterne set himself seriously to literary work, and from the ashes of the Political Romance arose *Tristram Shandy*.[63]

There is a strong suggestion that a connection between Yorick's paying the midwife's fee and Sterne's beginning a writing career is being darkly hinted at. Yorick pays for licensing of the midwife who later will appear at the birth of Tristram, the putative author of *Tristram Shandy*. Topham, who framed the license, was the occasion of the *Political Romance*, which was the cause of *Tristram Shandy*'s being written.

Admittedly, the indications that Sterne, as represented by

---
[61] *Ibid.*, pp. 12-13.
[62] *Tristram Shandy*, p. xxvii.
[63] *Ibid.*

Yorick, was implicated in the writing of *Tristram Shandy* are scarcely more than hints. But if Sterne, the minister, is to be kept apart from Tristram, the *persona*, they could not reasonably be presented in an obvious fashion.

In the second installment of *Tristram Shandy*, Yorick reappears. In the third, fourth, and final ones he becomes increasingly important. And in *A Sentimental Journey* he is the narrator hero. But in the beginning of *Tristram Shandy* he appears as a variously compounded figure of the fictive and the real who bears enough resemblance to the author to be identified with him. He is presented and then removed from the novel with a finality that leaves Tristram, the *persona*, nearly free from appearing to have any connection with Sterne the minister who was, of course, the actual writer.

In this chapter the attempt has been made to show not only that it would have been reasonable for Sterne the minister not to want to identify himself with a work like *Tristram Shandy* but also that Yorick was an agency by means of which the separation was nearly made. It was in keeping with the author's twenty years in the ministry that he should have come to certain convictions concerning the disparity between sacred and profane works and between the minister of the one and the writer of the other. And it is hard to believe that the curious-minded and well-read Sterne would have failed to give some thought to the matter. It is reasonable that when Sterne began writing *Tristram Shandy* he would have been influenced by the examples and the precepts (which he could scarcely have overlooked) of the older writers who had kept a greater distance between their works and themselves than Sterne's contemporary novelists. It is not surprising that the readers of the first installment of *Tristram Shandy* did not guess that it was the work of a minister. The last of this chapter has endeavored to show that Parson Yorick played an important part in establishing Tristram as the putative author.

Before the second installment of *Tristram Shandy* appeared, Sterne had identified himself much more closely with Yorick by publishing a volume of sermons as those of Mr. Yorick. He was also to find a way to bring Yorick back into the novel after having buried him. However, an examination of the matters important to Sterne later on is scarcely within the province of this chapter, which has been concerned with those important to him when he was writing the first installment of *Tristram Shandy*, when he was making the transition from minister to novelist.

V

THE NOVEL: FROM THE BEGINNING TO THE BIRTH AND THE MISNAMING OF TRISTRAM SHANDY

Although *Tristram Shandy* has been looked upon in this paper as primarily and preponderantly the product of Sterne's imagination, it also has been generally viewed as owing something to the author's life as a man, and insofar as the separation could be made, to the years as a minister. Now the novel will be considered mainly for its fictional and personal content and incidentally for what it reflects of the third and last phase of the author's life, the eight years in which Sterne wrote the five installments of *Tristram Shandy*. The present and the following chapters will endeavor to show that a significant change took place in the novel before it had been completed.

Chapter VI will deal with the latter portion of the work, that which begins with Tristram's statement made near the end of the second installment that he had completed a part of what he set out to write. The present chapter will be confined to the first part of the novel, that which begins with Tristram's begetting and ends with his birth and misnaming. And the high degree of fiction which pertained in the early part will be the chief consideration.

It has been maintained since the beginning of this paper that *Tristram Shandy* is much more a work of fiction than the older critics would have had it and slightly less than the pure work of the imagination that some of the modern critics would have it. In the second and third chapters of this paper, Sterne's life, particularly, the twenty years spent as a minister, was considered as having a determining effect on the content of the novel and on the way it was written.

Chapter IV dealt more narrowly with Sterne's separating the

novel from himself. It considered Sterne's ministry as a probable cause of his writing the novel as something apart from himself, and it also proposed that Yorick was an agency by which Sterne ensured his distinctness from and participation in the story. Although Chapter IV pointed out that Yorick would reappear and play an increasingly important part in the novel, it dealt with the presentation of Yorick in the first volume of *Tristram Shandy*, where, in the words of Willard Connelly, Sterne "deliberately buried himself as a parson". The conclusion was advanced that here Sterne used the narrative of the life and death of Yorick to separate himself from the putative author, Tristram.

The present chapter will generally review the two early installments of the novel in order to show that because of the highly complicated way in which Tristram was presented in the first part of the novel, very little of Sterne could have been included. More specifically, it will undertake to demonstrate that in the first two installments Tristram is presented as writing a kind of work which demands a certain degree of singularity in the writer; that he proposes to publish an eighty-volume work of his exceptional life and opinions, and to duplicate the actual life by equating writing time with historical time; that he is verifying the account of his prenatal perod by using peculiar documents and other individual materials; that he is relating the circumstances which might account for his being the odd creature that, even for a Shandy, he is; and that although he is writing as his odd inheritance has caused him to write, he is nevertheless trying to please the reader and to produce a work of lasting merit. Finally, the conclusion will be advanced that by the time Tristram writes how he had been born and named the fiction of the odd creature who is writing the book has been well established. Although Tristram declares he has "cleared the ground for his life and opinions", he has already written nearly all he is going to write about his life. He will have more to tell about the downfall of his father's systems, but those which Walter Shandy tried to put into practice in order to bring a certain kind of son into the world have all been told.

The major purpose of this chapter is to show that although in the later installments of the novel Sterne sometimes tended to confuse Tristram with himself, he had laid the groundwork so well that the entire work remained primarily and predominantly a novel or work of fiction, not Sterne's autobiography.

Under the circumstances, Tristram should have been a singular and highly complex character. Although after the novel was underway, Yorick appeared as a character who could be mistaken for Shakespeare's jester or for Sterne himself, at the beginning of the novel the narrator appeared as one who was more complex and less likely to be confused with others than Yorick. Naturally, a certain amount of complexity and distinctness was necessary for Tristram, even if he were to play no more than the role of the first person narrator. Percy Lubbock has said generally of the character who plays such a role:

The hero gives the story and indefeasable unity by the mere act of telling it. His career may not seem to hang together logically, artistically; but every part of it is at least united with every other part by the coincidence of its all belonging to one man.[1]

That Tristram functions in this fashion, and in others as well, is beginning to be recognized. In 1945, E. K. Russell observed that he was "as carefully portrayed as any of Sterne's people, and for as precise effect. He is the viewpoint of the novel".[2] Later on, John Traugott, as the title of his work partly denoted, considered that Tristram was the most important character in the novel. And in the introduction Traugott has specifically stated that every one of the other Shandys "does service as a 'voice' in Tristram's criss-crossed history of the human mind".[3] In 1952, Wayne C. Booth said that in reading *Tristram Shandy*, "our attention must be centered on the self-conscious narrator".[4] Recently, Walter Parrish has enlarged the function of Tristram: "As author,

---

[1] *The Craft of Fiction* (New York, Charles Scribner's Sons, n.d.), pp. 131 f.
[2] "*Tristram Shandy* and the Technique of the Novel", *SP*, XLII (1945), 584.
[3] *Tristram Shandy's World* (Berkeley and Los Angeles, University of California Press, 1954), p. xiii.
[4] "The Self-Conscious Narrator in Comic Fiction before *Tristram Shandy*", *PMLA*, LXVIII (1952), p. 165.

commentator, and narrator, he creates his own world and subjects it to his evaluating mind while telling it." [5] More recently, Wayne C. Booth has further enlarged the function by calling Tristram a vivid character, a creative writer and an influencer of events.[6] It must also be noticed that Alice Green Fredman has called attention to Tristram's role of experimental writer.[7]

Such statements are generally true of Tristram Shandy as he appears in the entire work, but they are more nearly true of him as he appears in the early installments of it. There, with emphasis on his own importance, he appears as a would-be creative writer who is composing an important part of his autobiography, the part in which he relates what occurred during the prenatal period of his existence.

Early in the first volume the narrator emphasizes the importance of himself as writer, as subject, and as object of the reader's concern. As a writer, he is endeavoring to do justice to himself and to the reader. The subject, himself, is so important that whatever remotely concerns it can be related. And the object of the reader's concern must be presented as being so important that the reader would not want to be denied anything which might enable him to understand what Tristram is and says. He writes:

I have undertaken, you see, to write not only my life, but my opinions also; hoping and expecting that your knowledge of my character, and of what kind of mortal I am, by the one would give you a better relish for the other ... then nothing which has touched me will be thought trifling in its nature or tedious in its telling.[8]

What importance the prenatal period has for the entire biography which is being projected is stated by Tristram after he has completed four volumes of it.

It is from this point properly that the story of my Life and Opinions sets out.... I have been but clearing the ground to raise the building

---

[5] "Twentieth-Century Criticism of Form in *Tristram Shandy*". Unpublished Ph.D. dissertation, Department of English, University of New Mexico (1959), p. 7.
[6] "Distance and Point of View", *Essays in Criticism*, X (1961), pp. 66-69.
[7] *Diderot and Sterne* (New York, Columbia University Press, 1955), pp. 130, 143.
[8] *Tristram Shandy*, pp. 10 f.

– and such a building do I foresee it will turn out, as never was planned, and as never was executed since Adam.⁹

And there are reasons to believe that a part of the novel has been written to "clear the ground" for a work longer than the completed one. It could run to eighty volumes. Tristram writes near the end of Volume I:

> I have constructed the main work and the adventitious parts of it with such intersections, and have so complicated and involved the digressive and progressive movements, one wheel within another, that the whole machine has been kept a-going; – and, what's more, it shall be kept a-going these forty years, if it pleases the fountain of good health to bless me so long with life and good spirits.¹⁰

According to Stephen Croft, a more moderate plan had been envisioned by Sterne: The author "was to travel his Hero Tristram Shandy all over Europe . . . and at length to return Tristram well informed and a complete English Gentleman".¹¹

In actuality, very little of the life of Tristram was written after the "ground had been cleared". One and a half volumes carried the account of his life up to the age of five, when the parents decided to put him into breeches and to get a male guardian for him. Except for an account of the journey Tristram made when he was in his forties, the biography was never resumed after it had been dropped in the middle of Volume VI. The remainder of the work was occupied mainly with the courtship of Uncle Toby and the Widow Wadman, and it ended about the time the hero was begotten. The degree to which Tristram was fictionally presented in the early installments, designed as prelude to a much longer account of himself, should have some bearing on the question of the degree to which he is primarily a fictional character.

We shall briefly notice the use of a device which calls the reader's attention to Tristram's being the subject and the writer. In the early part of the novel Tristram is presented as an autobiographer who assumes that he will spend an equal length of time in writing an account of his life to that he had spent in living it.

⁹ *Ibid.*, p. 336.
¹⁰ *Ibid.*, pp. 74 f.
¹¹ Quoted by Work, in *Tristram Shandy*, p. xlvi.

Alfred E. Lussky has observed that Sterne "keeps reminding the reader that the main goal of the author is to convey the exact truth, to preserve the strictest historical accuracy".[12] Actually, Sterne has Tristram remind the reader that such is the case. And Tristram tries to preserve historical accuracy not only in providing exact dates of certain events in his past but also in stating precisely when he is writing about the past.

In the first pages of *Tristram Shandy* the narrator carefully states that his begetting took place "in the night betwixt the first Sunday and the first Monday in the month of March, in the year of our Lord one thousand seven hundred and eighteen".[13] And on the following page, he writes that he was born "on the fifth day of November, 1718".[14]

Tristram is equally careful to state when the writing is taking place. And he is also concerned with maintaining a relation between the time of writing and the time he is writing about. Thirty-five pages after Tristram has stated the time of his geniture, he writes: "When my mother was three days, or thereabouts, gone with child, she began to cast her eyes upon the midwife, whom you have so often heard me mention; and before the week was well got round ... she had come to a final determination." On the same page Tristram says that he is "now writing this book for the edification of the world" on March 9, 1759.[15]

Further evidence of the effort to maintain the correspondence between the two times can be seen twenty pages later, where Tristram observes that it is "March 26, 1759, and between the hours of nine and ten in the morning".[16] In the meantime he had written about an approximately equal passage of time in the series of arguments, which appear to have continued for several nights before the matter was settled:

My father was for having the man-midwife by all means, – my mother by no means. ... What could my father do? He was almost at his

---

[12] *Tieck's Romantic Agony* (Chapel Hill, University of North Carolina Press, 1932), p. 160.
[13] *Tristram Shandy*, p. 8.
[14] *Ibid.*, p. 9.
[15] *Ibid.*, p. 44.
[16] *Ibid.*, p. 64.

wit's end; talked it over with her in all moods; – placed his arguments in all lights; – argued the matter with her like a christian, – like a heathen, – like a husband, – like a father, – like a patriot, – like a man: – my mother answered everything like a woman. . . . What could my mother do? She had the advantage (otherwise she had been certainly overpowered) of a small amount of chagrin personal at the bottom which bore her up, and enabled her to dispute the affair with my father to so equal an advantage – that both sides sung *Te Deum*. In a word, my mother was to have the old woman, – and the operator was to have the licence to drink a bottle of wine with my father and my uncle *Toby Shandy* in the back parlour, for which he was to be paid five guineas.[17]

Sterne evidently intended for the actual writing time of the first two volumes to conform to the fiction that Tristram was writing at the same pace he had lived. That such was his intention is indicated by the letter of May 23, 1759, to Robert Dodsley, the prospective printer of *Tristram Shandy*: "If you publish it now – a second volume will be ready by Christmas or Nov. – the reason for some such interval you will see in reading the book." [18] Considering that Tristram was begotten in the first week of March and born in November, that the first installment carried the prenatal life of Tristram up to the beginning of his mother's labor, and that the work was ready by Christmas, one can see that Sterne actually had kept the first installment fairly close to schedule.

Although the relation between the two kinds of time was more insisted upon and better carried through in the first installment than in the later ones, Tristram, even as late as Volume VII, occasionally reminds the reader that such had been his intentions in writing his autobiography. We shall notice what the scope of the intention was and how it was relinquished.

In the first volume Tristram presents himself as a writer who is unable to proceed at a faster rate than he is going and who has resigned himself to writing slowly. At the same time, he announces that he will write two volumes a year of his life every year, and if he "can make a tolerable bargain" with his bookseller, he will continue to do so as long as he lives.[19] Later on in the same volume,

[17] *Ibid.*, p. 48.
[18] *Letters*, p. 74.
[19] *Tristram Shandy*, p. 37.

he is more specific about the time required to complete the work: If he is blessed with health and good spirits, "the work will be kept a-going for forty years".[20] Since Sterne had presented Tristram as beginning the work at the age of forty, the reader might be led to believe that Tristram would spend the second forty years in writing about what had happened in the first forty. And in fact, in a later volume Tristram does say that his original intention was to spend a day of writing for each day he had lived.[21]

The time relationship is less insisted upon in the second installment. And it is abandoned in the third, where Tristram's life is accounted for to the age of five and then dropped to give an account of Uncle Toby's amours, which took place before Tristram's geniture. Although the two-volumes a year were published for three years, there was a three-year interval before Volumes VII and VIII were published. In the fourth installment even Uncle Toby's amours are interrupted to give an account of Tristram's flight from death. The fifth, or the final, installment consisted of only one volume. In it the story of the amours is resumed and concluded. And Uncle Toby's disillusionment, with which *Tristram Shandy* ends, takes place about the same time as that of Tristram's geniture.

It might even appear that the ralationship is being abandoned in the middle of Volume IV, when Tristram exclaims that he has been writing for a year since he has completed the first installment and has not got beyond the first day of his life.[22] Furthermore, Tristram has advanced the life only another day when he announces that except for one more chapter he has now completed the fourth volume.

What a rate I have gone on at, curvetting and frisking it away, two up and two down for four volumes together.... And so have got off, and here am I standing with my bridle in one hand, and with my cap in the other, to tell my story – And what is it? You shall hear in the next chapter.[23]

[20] *Ibid.*, p. 74.
[21] *Ibid.*, p. 285.
[22] *Ibid.*, p. 286.
[23] *Ibid.*, pp. 298 f.

A certain amount of conformity to the time relationship is nevertheless achieved when Volume IV has been completed. Besides the fact that the two volumes were produced on schedule, twelve more chapters, instead of one, were written, and the hero's life was carried on until the news of Bobby's death established Tristram as "heir-apparent to the Shandy family".[24] Tristram might well have been a year old by that time.

Although Sterne abandoned the writing time and living time of Tristram Shandy in the succeeding volumes, he proposed and fairly well sustained the fiction in the first installment and made some effort to carry it out in the second. Considering that the device emphasized Tristram's singularity, it is important in establishing the novel as primarily a work of fiction.

Brief notice will be taken of a phase of the authorial pose, which is emphasized at the beginning of *Tristram Shandy*, but is somewhat neglected after the first volume. It was offered as a practical explanation for Tristram's inability to relate more than a year of his life in a year of writing, but it also served to set Tristram apart from Sterne. The narrator presented himself as a forty-year-old writer, who, in reconstructing the period of his existence which would have been impossible for him to recall, was utilizing materials peculiar to himself, his family, and his locality.

Tristram complains that he cannot go any faster in this kind of writing:

He will have views and prospects to himself perpetually soliciting his eye, which he can no more help than standing still to look at than he can fly; he will moreover have various accounts to consider, anecdotes to pick up, inscriptions to make out, stories to weave in, traditions to sift, personages to call upon. . . . To sum up all; there are archives at every stage to be looked into, and rolls, records, documents, and endless genealogies, which justice ever and anon calls him back to stay the reading of.[25]

Immediately after Tristram has related the begetting scene in the first two chapters of the novel, he writes: "To my uncle Mr.

---

[24] *Ibid.*, p. 336.
[25] *Ibid.*, p. 37.

THE NOVEL: TO BIRTH AND MISNAMING OF TRISTRAM 111

Toby Shandy do I stand indebted for the preceding anecdote." In the fourth chapter, "another small anecdote known only in our own family", and a memorandum from his "father's pocketbook, which now lies upon the table" [26] are used to date his geniture. A few chapters later, in what is the greatest exhibit of all of his use of documents peculiar to the Shandy family, Tristram protests that he cannot "proceed further in this history" until he looks into his mother's marriage settlement. But he finds it, declares that he has studied it for "almost a day and half", and, then, reproduces it for the reader's benefit.[27]

In later volumes of *Tristram Shandy*, two or three family papers are referred to, but the reader's attention to Tristram's reliance upon them is less forcibly demanded. His great grandparents in Volume III are presented in the act of signing a marriage settlement, but there is no mention of Tristram's perusing the document.[28] And, when, in Volume IV, Tristram mentions Great-Aunt Dinah's legacy, the family's possession of the Ox-moor property, and the ruinous lawsuit, nothing is said about family records.[29]

Some of the other sources come from outside the Shandy family. Part of what the writer knows about Yorick has been obtained from Eugenius. Somehow Tristram has gained access to the records of the Yorick family, wherein he finds a copy of the midwife's license as well as the genealogy of the family. And, as we have noticed in Chapter IV of this paper, he quotes excerpts from them.

In Volume I the testimony of Eugenius, the midwife's license, and the Yorick genealogy are fabrications, and as such they are Tristram's. But by the middle of the second volume a difference between Sterne's and Tristram's materials has been indicated: Sterne's own sermon has been presented as being read aloud by Tristram's father and Corporal Trim. The following reasons are given for including it in the history:

The first is, That in doing justice, I may give rest to *Yorick's* ghost;

---

[26] *Ibid.*, pp. 8 f.
[27] *Ibid.*, pp. 36 f.
[28] *Ibid.*, pp. 217 f.
[29] *Ibid.*, pp. 332 f.

– which, as the country people, and some others, believe, – *still walks*. The second reason is, that by laying open this story to the world, I gain an opportunity of informing it, – That in case the character of parson *Yorick*, and this sample of his sermons is liked, – that there are now in the possession of the Shandy family, as many as will make a handsome volume, at the world's service, – and much good may they do it.[30]

One can also notice that in dealing with some of the other materials in *Tristram Shandy* Sterne changes his way of presenting them. In the early volumes Sterne insists upon the materials being genuine. Tristram presents the document of the "Docteurs de Sorbonne" on baptism and the words and music of Uncle Toby's song, "Lillibulero", in Chapters XX and XXI of Volume I; the sermon, "On Conscience", takes up twenty pages of Chapter XVII of Volume II; and the curse of Bishop Ernulphus, in Latin, with the English translation, takes up ten pages of Chapter XI of Volume III. All four of the transcriptions have been authenticated.[31] As in the case of the objective handling of time, there is less adherence to the actual in the later volumes. In them appear such works as the *Slawkenberglus Fabella* and the *Tristrapaedia*.[32]

In the early volumes of *Tristram Shandy* the narrator assumes the role of an autobiographer who calls attention to his careful use of materials that are peculiar to himself, his family, and his neighborhood. In the later volumes there is less obvious use of such procedure, although as Theodore Baird has pointed out, Sterne was careful to avoid anachronisms in all of *Tristram Shandy*.[33] In dealing with Yorick, however, who is closely related to Sterne, Tristram at first fabricates documents but later on uses a real sermon of Sterne's. The overall effect is that when in later volumes of the novel certain works are introduced, they have been made more acceptable and have more appearance of being genuine because they have been preceded by bona fide works.

In the first installment of *Tristram Shandy* the narrator has

[30] *Ibid.*, p. 143.
[31] *Ibid.*, pp. 58, n. 3, 69, n. 10, 142, n. 2, 170, n. 4.
[32] *Ibid.*, pp. 244-271, 390-398.
[33] "The Time-Scheme of *Tristram Shandy*", *PMLA*, LI (1936), pp. 803-820.

been set apart from Sterne and made a discreet character by several means: He has been presented as an autobiographer who assumes that his subject is important enough for him to spend forty years in writing about it. He is so peculiarly constituted that he must spend an equal amount of time in writing to that which he had lived. And he will write about the first part of his existence from documents that are peculiar to himself and about which the reader must be convinced of their authenticity.

But there is still another and more important way in which Tristram has been made a singular character. He is presented as an autobiographer who is aware of his own peculiar habits of thinking and who sets out to examine the circumstances in the early part of his existence which might have been responsible for making him the kind of thinker he is. It seems likely that the way he will write his account has already been predetermined by what had happened in the early part of his life. In such an involved situation there is scarcely a place for anyone except Tristram Shandy to be the writer.

That Tristram is working in this manner may be seen in the opening paragraph of Volume I, where he says that the reader must wait to see if the accident at conception has had any ill-effect on the narrator: "I am verily persuaded I should have made quite a different figure in the world, from that in which the reader is likely to see me."

In the second chapter, Tristram decides that the accident had not done any physical harm to the "homunculus":

Now, dear Sir, what if any accident had befallen him in his way alone? − or through terror of it, natural to so young a traveller, my little gentlemen had got to his journey's end miserably spent; − his muscular strength and virility miserably worn to a thread.... I tremble to think what a foundation had been laid for a thousand weaknesses both of body and mind, which no skill of the physician or the philosopher could ever afterwards have set thoroughly to rights.

In the third chapter, Tristram recalls that his father and his uncle believed that he was a strange sort of person, even as a Shandy, and that they believed the accident at the moment of generation had been responsible for his oddity:

To my uncle Mr. *Toby Shandy* do I stand Indebted for the preceding anecdote, to whom my father ... had oft, and heavily, complained of the injury.... He said his heart all along foreboded and he saw it verified in this [Tristam's way of setting up a top], and a thousand and other observations he had made upon me, That I should never think nor act like any other man's child: *But alas!* continued he... *My Tristam's misfortunes began nine months before he came into the world.*

In the fourth chapter Tristram comes to a decision about how the accident had affected him. He is not suffering from anything that happened to the "homunculus" in transit; but he is different from anyone else because he has inherited a certain way of thinking from his mother. And the mother's condition, that he has inherited, had been brought about by his father's regular habit of winding the clock and taking care of some little family concernments on the first Sunday night of every month:

It was attended but with one misfortune, which in a great measure, fell upon myself, and the effects of which I fear I shall carry with me to the grave; namely, that from an unhappy association of ideas which have no connection in nature, it so fell out at length, that my poor mother could never hear the clock wound up, – but the thoughts of some other things unavoidably popped into her head, – & *vice versa*: which strange combination of ideas, the sagacious *Locke*, who understood the nature of these things better than most men, affirms to have produced more wry actions than all the other sources of prejudice whatever.[34]

Although John Laird has observed that "Tristram's first piece of bad luck was an unfortunate association of ideas in his parents at the time of his begetting", it is evident that Tristram says the association of ideas was in the mind of only one parent, the mother, and her acquired habit has been passed on to her son, who, in writing an account of his life and opinions, is prone to combine all sorts of strange ideas.

Laurence Putney has seen this tendency in Tristram as responsible for the way a great deal of the novel was written:

---

[34] "Shandean Philosophy", in *Philosophical Excursions into English Literature* (Cambridge, Cambridge University Press, 1946), pp. 86 f.

The assumption of Tristram's mind provides also the chief structural device of the book.... Up to chapter xx of Volume VI, the misadventures of Tristram's life provide the skeleton on which the digressions are hung, and his is the mind so lost in the flux of thought, as explained by Locke's theory of the association of ideas, that each mischance he suffers leads into tangential mazes.[35]

Such a statement of Tristram's method of writing is true in part. He does indeed, as Putney has pointed out, write in what appears to be an aimless fashion:

Mrs. Shandy's ill-timed question leads to a discussion of the right of the homunculus, to the date of the conception, and to Walter's theory of geniture. The date of his conception involves its method, and that brings in the local midwife, whose existence in the neighborhood requires a description of Parson Yorick and his reasons for establishing the old woman in her vocation. Her role in Tristram's misfortunes would be inexplicable, in view of Dr. Slop's proximity, without a knowledge of his mother's marriage settlement. Tristram's name results in an exposition of Walter's theory of names with the history of Aunt Dinah, and Tristram's quasi-logical comment that one cannot be christened before one is born reminds him of the doctors of the Sorbonne on that subject. While Walter and Toby are awaiting Tristram's birth, they begin a discussion of Mrs. Shandy's reasons for rejecting Dr. Slop which cannot be understood until Uncle Toby's character has been elucidated. The accident to Tristram's nose is responsible for Walter's theory of the importance of noses with the reasons thereof and an account of his collection of books on the subject. From his favorite work the tale of Slawkenbergius is gleaned. The remainder of the fourth volume follows from the mistake at the christening which reaches its culmination in the ludicrous happenings at the Visitation Dinner.[36]

There is reason to believe that an explanation of Tristram's way of thinking and the way the first part of the novel is written must take some other things into account, and that when they are considered Tristram will be better revealed as a unique character and as one who is set apart from Laurence Sterne. We shall try to show that Tristram is presented as having inherited also some-

[35] "Laurence Sterne: Apostle of Laughter", in *The Age of Johnson: Essays Presented to Chauncey Brewster Tinker* (New Haven, Yale University Press, 1949), p. 162.
[36] *Ibid.*, pp. 163 f.

thing of his father's way of thinking, which, although it is wrong-headed, is not aimless. And we shall also try to show that Tristram continues writing "The Life and Opinions of Tristram Shandy, Gentleman", until he has presented a full account of his father's efforts to influence his character, and that the account comprises the first part of the novel.

Lehman has observed that Tristram has inherited the ways of thinking of both parents: "Tristram is the son in the flesh of a woman who cannot catch an implication and a man who tortures all reality to fit a hypothesis." [37] Putney has said that "Tristram's taste for the oddities of knowledge, his unpredictable attitudes toward persons and things rival his father's... Besides he has hypotheses of his own." [38]

It is not unreasonable to believe that Tristram is presenting himself as a writer who has inherited paradoxical capacities. He has inherited the faculty of associating random ideas from his mother, and that of "systematick" reasoning from his father. "The machinery of my work", says Tristram, "is of a species by itself; two contrary notions are introduced into it and reconciled, which are thought to be at variance with each other. In a word, my work is digressive, – and it is progressive too, – and at the same time." [39] Wayne Booth insists that the progressive and "systematick" side of Tristram's writing has been overlooked because it is repeated so less frequently, and seems so thoroughly confuted by everything he [Tristram] does.[40]

John Laird has well summarized the character of Walter Shandy:

There is no doubt about this. Mr. Walter Shandy was 'a philosopher in grain, speculative, systematical.' In the coach to London he 'would do nothing but syllogize within himself for a stage or two together.' He had 'extensive views of things.' Like all extensive systematic reasoners he would move both heaven and earth, and twist and torture everything in nature to support a hypothesis. 'What is the character

---

[37] "Of Time, Personality, and the Author", *University of Califorina Publications in English*, VIII (1941), p. 250.
[38] Putney, p. 165.
[39] *Tristram Shandy*, p. 73.
[40] Booth, p. 177.

of a family to an hypothesis?' he would ask when he supported his views by citing the awful example of 'my aunt Dinah' and the coachman.[41]

And one can see that Tristram in several instances is like his father. "My father was an excellent natural philosopher and much given to close reasoning upon the smallest matters", writes Tristram immediately after he himself has indulged in the same kind of reasoning about the effect the interruption might have had on the "homunculus". After Tristram has indulged in some more of the same kind of reasoning, he asks the reader to give him credit for a little more wisdom than appears upon his outside.[42] There is a closer resemblance to Walter Shandy in another self appraisal: "My way is ever to point out to the curious, different tracts of investigations, to come at the first springs of the events I tell." [43] After Tristram has described the amazement of the tutors at Jesus College when they observed Walter's facile use of logic, Tristram not only advances an hypothesis of his own to account for his father's skill in systematic reasoning but also sets himself up as a logician and as one who has invented a "name to be thrown into the treasury of the *Ars Logica*".[44] Tristram furthermore insists that his own writing is more orderly than it might appear to be:

> Tho' my digressions are all fair as you observe, – and that I fly off from what I am about, as far and as often too as any writer in Great-Britain; yet I take care to order my affairs so, that my main business does not stand still in my absence.[45]

And Tristram comes close to stating that he and his father are alike in hypothesis making. At the conclusion of the curse of Bishop Ernulphus Tristram writes:

> For this reason my father would oft-times affirm, there was not an oath ... which not to be found in Ernulphus. – In short, he would add, – I defy a man to swear out of it.

[41] Laird, p. 82.
[42] *Tristram Shandy*, p. 11.
[43] *Ibid.*, p. 66.
[44] *Ibid.*, pp. 53, 71.
[45] *Ibid.*, p. 72.

The hypothesis is like most of my father's, singular and ingenious too; – nor have I any objections to it, but that it overturns my own.[46]

Finally, Tristram was Walter's son in being a writer. The elder Shandy was the author of at least three works. One had been written several years before Tristram's birth: "He had wrote the Life of *Socrates* himself the year before he left off trade, which, I fear, was the means of hastening him out of it." And Sterne has Tristram say in a note: "This book my father would never consent to publish; 'tis in manuscript, with some other tracts of his, in the family, all or most of which will be printed in due time." [47] Tristram says of another work: "In the year sixteen, which was two years before I was born, he was at the pains of writing an express dissertation simply upon the word *Tristram*, shewing the world, with great candour and modesty, the grounds of his great abhorence to the name." [48] And after Bobby's death Walter began the *Tristra-paedia*, a system of education for Tristram, "at which he was three years and something more, indefatigably at work".[49]

That Tristram intends to write an account of his father's efforts to influence the son's character may be seen fairly early in the novel. After Tristram has introduced Walter's theory of the magic bias of proper names and aversion to the name of Tristram, he writes:

When this story is compared with the title-page, – will not the gentle reader pity my father from his soul? to see an orderly and well-disposed gentleman, who tho' singular, – yet inoffensive in his notions, – so played upon in them by cross purposes; – to look down upon the stage, and see him baffled and overthrown in all his little systems and wishes; to behold a train of events perpetually falling out against him, and in so critical and cruel a way, as if they had been planned and pointed against him merely to insult his speculations.[50]

What Walter's "first three great casts" for Tristram were can be seen after the account has been written. They were efforts to control circumstances in order that the son would have a proper

[46] *Ibid.*, p. 183.
[47] *Ibid.*, p. 368.
[48] *Ibid.*, p. 55.
[49] *Ibid.*, p. 55.
[50] *Ibid.*, pp. 372-375.

geniture, a well-shaped nose, and a good name. The reader is informed at the beginning of the work that the first cast had failed. Fifteen chapters later Tristram foretells that he has been doomed to have his nose mashed flat to his face. And in the nineteenth chapter he adds that he will be given the name for which his father felt the greatest aversion.

The narrator will, however, inform the reader how these disappointments to Walter came about. And he will do so in part as the son of Elizabeth Shandy, who has been conditioned to associate random ideas, and in part as the son of Walter Shandy, who has inherited a bent for systematic reasoning. He will be tempted into making digressions. At times he will be able to resist them. He restrains himself from telling about how the misnaming occurred: "If it was not necessary that I should be born before I was christened, I would this moment give the reader an account of it." [51] A few chapters later, he does not try to resist: "I have a strong propensity to begin this chapter nonsensically, and I will not balk my fancy. – Accordingly I set off thus." [52] And off he goes into speculating about the advantages of character delineation on the planet Mercury.

After the narrator has finally, in Volume IV, narrated the last of the "embryotic evils", how he had been misnamed, he calls special attention to Walter's summary of disappointments by entitling it "My Father's Lamentations". The Jeremiad reveals that although the writer had "flown off" from what he had been about "as far and as often too as any writer in Great-Britain", he had nevertheless taken care to order his affairs so that his main business had not stood still. How thoroughly the narrative had been "planned and pointed against" the father's efforts to apply for the benefit of the son the favorite theories of geniture, obstetrics, noses, and names may be seen in the opening sentences of the "Lamentation":

It is in vain longer ... to struggle as I have done against this most uncomfortable of human persuasions – I see it plainly ... that heaven has thought fit to draw its heaviest artillery against me; and that the

[51] *Ibid.*, p. 56.
[52] *Ibid.*, p. 74.

prosperity of my child is the point of which the whole force has been brought to bear. Unhappy *Tristram*! child of wrath! child of decrepitude! interruption! mistake! and discontent! What one misfortune in the book of embryotic evils, that could unmechanize thy frame, or entangle thy filaments! which had not fallen upon thy head, or ever thou comest into the world – what evils in thy passage into it! What evils since! [53]

Walter then proceeds to enumerate the course of the disasters. The interruption at the time of conception had "dispersed, confused, confounded, scattered, and sent to the devil' the animal spirits, with which "memory, fancy, and quick parts should have been conveyed".

"Here then was the time to put a stop to this persecution against him; – and to try an experiment at least", continued Walter. But Mrs. Shandy had refused to submit to any kind of regimen while she was carrying the child. And she had "fumed inwardly" and disturbed the foetus by wanting to "lie in at town".

Mrs. Shandy had furthermore blocked all her husband's efforts to preserve the apex of the infant's head from damage. She had refused to have the child born by a Caesarean operation or to have Dr. Slop, who might have delivered the child by the feet. "Tis ninety *per Cent*. insurance, that the fine network of the intellectual web be not rent and torn to a thousand tatters."

Two more misfortunes were still to come to the infant Tristram and to Walter's schemes for him: the broken nose and the name of Tristram:

– Still we could have done. – Fool, coxcomb, puppy – give him but a NOSE ... fate might have done her worst. Still Brother *Toby*, there was one dye left for our child after all – O *Tristram! Tristram! Tristram!*

After Walter's "Lamentation" Tristram observes that he now stands with his bridle in his hands waiting to tell his story. And he does carry the events of his life up to the time of Bobby's death in Volume IV. But after the misnaming he begins to neglect the story of his own life. By the middle of Volume VI he brings himself up to the age of five, when he had been accidentally circum-

---

[53] *Ibid.*, p. 296.

cised. He then concerns himself with the love affair of Uncle Toby and the Widow Wadman, which had taken place before he had been conceived.

Up to this place in the narrative Tristram has been concerned primarily with the circumstances of his prenatal existence and Walter Shandy's ineffectual efforts to control them. The writer appears to have inherited certain ways of thinking from his parents; but in spite of all the systems the father might raise to account for his son's peculiar character, even as a Shandy, Tristram has found little within the first nine months of his life that can be held responsible for the kind of creature he is. He has, however, demonstrated, as Lehman has observed of him, "that if you keep expanding a hypothesis to fit the facts you presently have no hypothesis at all . . . you have only nature".[54]

Before notice is taken of the extent to which "all of" Walter Shandy's "little systems and wishes" were handled in the first two installments of the novel, another phase of Tristram's authorial pose must be briefly examined. It is that of the experimental writer, who is anxious that his work be regarded as a successful literary endeavor. Such a pose could permit a great deal of Laurence Sterne himself to be presented in the narrator, but Tristram is presented as one whose method of composition is peculiar to himself. He has a Shandean hypothesis about character drawing: "In a word", says Tristram, 'I will draw my uncle Toby's character from his hobby-horse." [55] And something of the same kind of drawing will suffice for Uncle Toby's servant, Corporal Trim, who "besides what he gained Hobby-Horsically, as a body servant" became "Hobby-Horsical *per se*".[56] Tristram's hypothesis for the effectiveness of the method is "that if you are able to give a clear description of the nature of the one, you may form a pretty exact notion of the genius and the character of the other".[57] He assumes that he can relate any detail about himself that he wishes and the reader will be interested in it if he can

---

[54] B. H. Lehman, "Comedy and Laughter", in *Five Gayley Lectures* (Berkeley and Los Angeles, University of California Press, 1954), p. 94.
[55] *Tristram Shandy*, p. 77.
[56] *Ibid.*, p. 95.
[57] *Ibid.*, p. 11.

introduce himself and "the slight acquaintance terminate in friendship".[58] He advances the theory that writing is like whistling a tune. And he will write as Walter's son, who tortures reality into systems, and as Elizabeth's, who writes whatever he happens to think about.

Despite his writing as he has been conditioned, Tristram evinces concern for the reader's approval. Throughout the first two installments such phrases appear as "Either laugh with me, or at me, only keep your temper"; "How this event came about shall be laid before the reader in due time"; and "I do all that lies in my power to keep his [the reader's] imagination as busy as my own." But what appears to be genuine concern comes in the "Author's Preface", inserted in Chapter XX of Volume III:

> No, I'll not say a word about it, – here it is; – in publishing it, – I have appealed to the world, – and to the world I leave it; – it must speak for itself. All I know of the matter is, – that when I sat down, my intent was to write a good book; and as far as the tenuity of my understanding would hold out, a wise, aye, and discreet, – taking care, only as I went along, to put into it all the wit and the judgment (be it more or less) which the great author and the bestower of them had thought fit originally to give me, so that, as your worships see, – 'tis just as God pleases.[59]

After Tristram has told the story of his birth and misnaming, he looks back over what he has written and says in defense of it:

> "Albeit, gentle reader, I have lusted earnestly, and endeavoured carefully (according to the measure of such slender skill as God has vouchsafed me...) that these little books which I here put into thy hands, may stand instead of bigger books." [60]

In the final chapter of Volume IV, he repeats that he has completed four volumes of the work and explains that 'True Shandeism opens the heart and the lungs" and "makes the wheel of life run long and cheerfully round". He then concludes the chapter with confidence that the reader will want more of his kind of writing. He also gives some warning that the ensuing volumes

---

[58] *Ibid.*, p. 11.
[59] *Ibid.*, p. 192.
[60] *Ibid.*, p. 43.

will be different; that is, if he lives to write them. And here Sterne almost drops the mask, for Tristram's writing depends upon Sterne's living.

I would add to my prayers that may God make you wise as well as merry.... And so with this moral for the present, may it please your worships and your reverences, I take my leave of you this twelvemonth, when (unless this vile cough kills in the meantime) I'll have another pluck at your beards, and lay open a story to the world you little dream of.

Although the story Tristram lives to tell hurries through the first five years and then takes up the account of Uncle Toby's amours, several matters begun in the first two installments are continued. For one, Tristram had not finished with his father's schemes, which are important enough that E. A. Baker has seen Tristram as "merely a peg for his father's absurd philosophy".[61]

In returning to the way the narrator deals with "all of his father's little systems and wishes", it should be noticed that in the first four volumes only those have been overthrown which Walter had tried to put into practice on Tristram the embryo. The subsequent volumes will offer further explanations of his theories of names and noses, and the final volume will reveal that even before Tristram was begotten circumstances had already proved to everyone but Walter that some of his theories were untenable. "My father was a gentleman of many virtues", says Tristram early in the first volume, "but he had a strong spice of that in his temper which might, or might not, be added to that number. – 'Tis known by the name of perseverance in a good cause and obstinacy in a bad one." [62] All the way through the novel, circumstances may hinder or invalidate his hypotheses, but they will never cause him to lose his faith in them. Walter Shandy is, as Edwin Muir has said of Uncle Toby, "beyond time and change".[63]

Walter's belief in the dominant role of the male in procreation is repeatedly challenged by the time Tristram has been born. In fact, in the year before Tristram was begotten Mrs. Shandy's false

---

[61] *History of the Novel* (New York, Barnes & Noble, 1950), IV, p. 255.
[62] *Tristram Shandy*, p. 43.
[63] *The Structure of the Novel* (London, Hogarth Press, 1946), p. 81.

pregnancy had made Walter uncomfortable. "Nothing in the whole affair provoked him so much as the condolences of his friends and the figure they would both make in church the first *Sunday*." [64] Tristram has already revealed what the first Sunday night in each month signified for his father.

There is more than a suggestion that Walter's assumption of masculine superiority was challenged on the night Tristram was born. Elizabeth's maid Susannah would scarcely deign to answer Walter's questions:

— And how does your mistress? Cried my father.... As well, said *Susannah*, tripping by, as could be expected.... And how is the child, pray? — No answer. And where is Dr. Slop? added my father, raising his voice aloud and looking over the ballusters — Susannah was out of hearing.[65]

That Walter feels his position as a male has been treated with contempt is evident from his ensuing conversation with Uncle Toby:

From the very moment the mistress of the house is brought to bed, every female in it, from my lady's gentlewoman down to the cinderwinch, becomes an inch taller for It, and give themselves more airs upon that single inch, than all their other inches put together.

I think rather, replied my uncle *Toby*, that 'tis we who sink an inch lower....

God bless ⎱ 'em all — said my uncle Toby and my
Duce take ⎰ father, each to himself.

It is not however until Chapter XXXII of Volume V that Walter's argument for male superiority in general receives its most serious set back. It has been demonstrated by Wilfred Watson that Corporal Trim unmistakably does so by honoring his mother as well as his father in repeating the catechism, and by giving a reason that Walter cannot overthrow.[66] It will be shown in Chapter VI of this paper that the most serious challenge to Walter's assumption of male superiority comes at the end of the novel when

---

[64] *Tristram Shandy*, p. 43.
[65] *Ibid.*, p. 284.
[66] Wilfred Watson, "The Fifth Commandment: Some Allusions to Sir Robert Filmer's Writings in *Tristram Shandy*", *MLN*, LXII (1947), pp. 234-240.

the Shandy bull has been found inadequate. Since, however, the event took place before Tristram's geniture, it cannot be viewed as culminating the attacks on Walter's position.

In the first four volumes of the novel Tristram's father has at least an equal amount of difficulty in persuading the other members of the Shandy family to share any of his convictions or to act upon them. His wife, his brother, and his wife's maid are able in almost every case to have their way and to thwart him.

Even Mrs. Shandy, of whom he complains that she will not argue at all, is able to defeat him. There is no doubt about the issue of the debate over the midwife:

My father begged and intreated she would once recede from her prerogative in this matter and suffer him to choose for her, – my mother, on the contrary, insisted upon her privilege in this matter, to choose for herself, and to have no mortalls help but the old woman's. What could my father do?

He fares no better in attempting to persuade her to have the child delivered by a Caesarean operation:

He mentioned the thing one afternoon to my mother, – merely as a matter of fact; – but seeing her turn pale as ashes at the very mention of it, as much as the operation flattered his hopes, – he thought it well to content himself with admiring – what he thought was no purpose to propose.

In several cases Uncle Toby proves himself to be a better rhetorician than his brother; he prevails on him to allow Trim to make mortars out of the ancestral jackboots, to finance the war games, and to employ Le Fever's son as Tristram's tutor. In fact, not one instance is recorded of Uncle Toby's failing to have his way with his brother.

The talkative Susannah baffles Walter and finally defeats his plans for having the child named "Trismegistus". But it appears that loquacity is not the only weapon she uses against him. When she first appears on the scene in Volume II, he remarks that "she is running as if they were going to ravish her". When, in Volume III, she comes downstairs to summon Dr. Slop to deliver the child, her way of handling the man midwife reveals something of her power:

– Bless my soul! – my poor mistress is ready to faint, and her pains are gone, – and the drops are done, – and the bottle of julap is broke, – and the nurse has cut her arm, ... and the child is where it was continued *Susannah*, – and the midwife has fallen backwards upon the edge of the fender and bruised her hip as black as your hat. – I'll look at it quoth Dr. *Slop*. There is no need of that, replied *Susannah*, – you had better look at my mistress, – but the midwife would gladly first give you an account of how things are, so desires you would go upstairs and speak to her this moment.

When she appears again, in Volume IV and after Tristram has been born, she catches Walter's attention by hurrying past him carrying a huge pincushion. Whatever significance the pincushion has for him, it is plain enough that he tries to engage her in conversation and is silenced.[67]

And when Susannah walks into his bedroom to ask what the child will be named, Walter, despite his earlier anounced intentions for naming his son, places the name of "Trismegistus" in the balance with that of "Toby'. He then asks her to hand him his breeches, but she refuses. She next excites him by leaving a comparison unfinished: "The child is as black as my – As your what? said my father, for like all orators, he was a deep searcher into comparisons." He then weighs the relative advantages of the names and decides upon "Trismegistus". But he wonders if since Susannah is "a leaky vessel", she can carry the name.

When Walter arrives at the scene of the christening, the name of "Tristram" has already been given the child. Even then, if he had remained long enough to learn the true state of affairs, he might have changed the name; but his breeches come unbuttoned. According to the Hogarth drawing, which Sterne requested and must have approved, Susannah stared intently at the cause of the squire's discomfiture. "My father cried Pish! He whisked himself about – and with his breeches held up by one hand ... he returned along the gallery to bed."

A few chapters later Walter Shandy will learn that his child has been named "Tristram". He will then utter his "Lamentations", in which he lists the calamities that have befallen the child "in the book of embryotic evils", and which since it concerns

[67] *Tristram Shandy*, p. 284.

Walter as well as Tristram is an apt description of what we have called "the first part of *Tristram Shandy*". Beyond this point in the novel Tristram will carry forward the account of his life up to the fifth year, and he will then abandon it. Before he leaves off the story of his own life to take up the account of Uncle Toby's amours, he will write of his becoming the Shandy heir and of his having the window accident. He will also write of his father's efforts to write a system of education for him and of the decision to put him into breeches and under the care of a male guardian. But Tristram's life after birth will not be completed. The prenatal life of Tristram and Walter's efforts to influence it has however been completed when Walter learns that the child has been named "Tristram", the capstone of all the embryotic evils.

It is obvious that we have considered Walter's theories and efforts on the behalf of Tristram as second only in importance to the life of Tristram in the first two installments. Where James Aiken Work has considered that this part of the novel deals primarily with "Walter Shandy and his household",[68] and Wayne C. Booth that it deals with "the infant Tristram, before and after birth",[69] it has seemed more reasonable to agree in part with each: to consider Tristram as being primarily important and Walter as being no less than secondarily so.

In this chapter the conclusion has been advanced that Tristram Shandy as a fictive autobiographer should be understood as a discrete character and writer. Although his actual singularity and separateness from Sterne is coming to be recognized, certain devices by which the fiction is established in the first two installments have not been adequately recognized. It has been pointed out that Tristram proposed and maintained in the early part of the novel that his life was singular enough to furnish materials for many volumes, which he must write as the same rate he had lived, and that he must establish the reality of it by utilizing his own peculiar sources of information.

We have contended that in the first part of *Tristram Shandy* Tristram is also presented as relating the odd circumstances which

---

[68] *Tristram Shandy*, p. xlix.
[69] Booth, p. 177.

might account for his own oddity as a man and as a writer, and that although he writes as he believes his strange nature compels him, he is anxious to please the reader and to have his work "swim down the gutter of time".

We have also tried to show that Tristram had so well established the fiction of himself and of his strange father by the time he had told of his birth and misnaming that in spite of taking up the affairs of Uncle Toby and of coming close to being Laurence Sterne, *Tristram Shandy* remained primarily and preponderantly a work of fiction by the fictive writer, Tristram.

How the writing is handled in the later installments will be considered in the next chapter.

VI

THE NOVEL: FROM THE BEGINNING TO THE FINAL COMMENT OF YORICK

In the review of the course of Sterne criticism in the first chapter of this study, it appeared that both author and work might be better understood and evaluated if *Tristram Shandy* were regarded as primarily a fictional construct on which the life and ministry of the author had exercised some influence. Accordingly, the second and third chapters examined, insofar as they could be separated, the life and the ministry of Laurence Sterne for their probable effect on the way he wrote *Tristram Shandy*. Strong indications were found that Sterne's formal education and reading, his ministry with its sermon preparation and delivery, and his view of man and art that being a minister could bring about – all in some measure had been responsible for what the novel came to be.

The fourth chapter weighed the probability of the author's using the short narrative of the life and death of Yorick as a device to separate himself from the novel and especially from the hero-narrator if it, Tristram. The study of the presentation of Yorick furnished reason to believe that Sterne had used it to separate Tristram from himself and that something of his method of handling structure could be learned from it. The two black pages at the conclusion of the account were not only emblems of Yorick's passing but also signified that a part of the novel had been completed.

On the assumption that Sterne had separated himself from Tristram and was presenting him as writing in a fashion consonant with the character of Tristram, a study was made in the fifth chapter of Walter's efforts to bring an excellent son into the world and of Tristram's efforts to present an account of Walter, Walter's efforts, and himself as Walter's disappointment. Evidence was found that although the series, or sequence, of events contained interpolations and other sequences of events, the reciprocally creative efforts of Walter and Tristram began in the first paragraph with the begetting scene and ended in the middle of the fourth volume with Walter's "Lamentations" and Tristram's avowal of change of topic.

The present chapter will conclude the study of the man and the minister and the novelist and the novel by further examining the work itself. Other parts of the novel will be surveyed. And an attempt will be made to find a relation of the parts of the novel to the whole work. The last two chapters will be particularly studied for the meaning they might have for the whole novel, for the hero and the narrator, and for the actual author. Finally, brief notice will be given to Yorick, who becomes increasingly prominent at the end of the novel, makes the last comment in it, and next appears as the hero of Sterne's other novel, *A Sentimental Journey*.

That *Tristram Shandy* has enough form to merit the study of its whole and parts is not a view radically different from that which now is held by several Sterne critics. Although a century ago Walter Bagehot declared that "*Tristram Shandy*, being indeed a book without plan or order, is in every generation unfit for analysis",[1] this generation, despite some disagreement about what the plan and the order is, has been able to subject the novel to analysis.

Analyses of *Tristram Shandy* have depended to a certain extent on the way critics have regarded Tristram's self-conscious comments. The apparently contradictory nature of Tristram's comments about the way he is writing has long been a problem. Tristram, on the one hand, will write "Ask my pen – it governs me"[2] or "I begin with writing the first sentence – and trusting

---

[1] "Sterne and Thackery", in *Literary Studies of Walter Bagehot*, "Introduction" by George Sampson (London and New York, J. M. Dent & E. P. Dutton, 1911), II, p. 104.
[2] *Tristram Shandy*, p. 416.

to Almighty God for the second"; [3] on the other, he will write "my work is digressive and progressive too" [4] or "Every circumstance relating to it in its proper place shall be faithfully laid before you".[5]

Where the earlier critics generally tended to accept Tristram's avowals of lack of purpose and to reject his declarations of purpose, the modern critics have reversed the procedure. H. K. Russell and Dorothy Van Ghent, for example, have tended to discount Tristram's denial of purpose. As far back as 1942, Russell decided that in the following case Tristram's invocation to "the powers" for aid was ironic.[6] Tristram had exclaimed:

O ye powers (for powers ye are and great ones too) — which enable mortal man to tell a story worth the telling; that kindly shew him, where he is to begin it, — and where he is to end it, and what he is to put into it, — and what he is to leave out, — how much of it he is to cast into the shade, and whereabouts he is to throw his light! ye who preside over this vast empire of biographical freebooters, and see how many scrapes and plunges your subjects hourly fall into; — will you do one thing?

I beg and beseech you (in the case you will do nothing better for us) that wherever, in any part of your dominions it so falls out that three roads meet in one point, ... that at least you set up a guide post in the center of them, in mere charity to direct *an uncertain devil* [italics mine], which of the three he is to take.[7]

In 1953, Dorothy Van Ghent cautioned those who would study *Tristram Shandy* "not to take this authorial cry of distress for uncertainty; for it is one of the false scents Sterne lays down humoristically in order to give his work the appearance of artlessness and primitive spontaniety".[8]

Tristram's statements of serious intentions have been championed, especially by Wayne C. Booth and Rufus D. Putney. Although Putney's statements about the matter came first, Booth has been stronger in contending for their serious nature. Booth,

---

[3] *Ibid.*, p. 540.
[4] *Ibid.*, p. 72.
[5] *Ibid.*, p. 67.
[6] *Tristram Shandy and the Technique of the Novel*, p. 590.
[7] *Tristram Shandy*, p. 207.
[8] *The English Novel: Form and Function*, p. 88.

in the essay, "Did Sterne Complete *Tristram Shandy?*" wrote: "In practically every case of Tristram's irresponsibility as far as narrative devices are concerned, the reader finds himself fooled; the caprice is not caprice after all." [9] Booth contends, furthermore, that Sterne not only showed a concern for form by way of the comments but succeeded in composing a well-constructed novel. "If one forgets the traditional attacks, one finds every reason to believe that Sterne worked not only with care to tie the major episodes together but that with the ninth volume, he completed the novel as he had originally conceived it." [10]

Booth's plea for recognition of the valuable nature of the commentary and of the extent of the form in the novel was derived in part from an article by Putney, who had found an indication of partial structure in Chapter XX of Volume VI of *Tristram Shandy*. Tristram had written:

> We are now going to enter upon a new scene of events. – Leave we then the breeches in the taylor's hands, with my father standing over him with his cane, ... Leave we my mother – (truest of all the *Pococurante's* of her sex!)! ... Leave we *Slop* likewise to the full profit of all my dishonours. – Leave we poor *Le Fever* to recover, and get home the best he can. – And last of all, – because the hardest of all – Let us leave, if possible, myself: – But 'tis impossible, – I must go along with you to the end of the work.[11]

For Putney, the passage marked the departure from the plan adhered to for five and a half volumes. "Up to this point", he argued, "*Tristram Shandy* is as carefully constructed as *Tom Jones*." [12] Sterne had changed the novel, he believed, not because his first plan had become inadequate, but because he could no longer resist "the clamor against the double entendre and the downright indecencies of the second installment [Volumes III and IV]".[13] Putney looked upon the change as having serious consequences:

[9] *MP*, XLVIII (1951), p. 173.
[10] *Ibid.*, p. 181, n. 18.
[11] *Tristram Shandy*, p. 442.
[12] Laurence Sterne, "Apostle of Laughter", in *The Age of Johnson* (New Haven, Yale University Press), p. 165.
[13] *Ibid.*, p. 164.

The abandonment of the scheme in the middle of Volume VI for the interpolation of Uncle Toby's wars, his amours with the Widow Wadman, and Tristram's travels has obscured the structural unity, ... that prevailed for the first five and a half volumes.[14]

Although Wayne Booth in other cases has been more insistent than Putney on accepting Tristram's commentary for what it says, in this case he would disregard it and extend the structure to embrace the entire novel.

There is no real shift in the direction to match the announced shift in the sixth volume. The details of Uncle Toby's campaigns and amours have been promised again and again, beginning in Volume I, and the misfortunes of Tristram's youth pervade the remainder of the book (to say nothing of the fact which Putney does *not* notice) – that Tristram, the adult narrator, persists fully as much after the shift as before.[15]

Despite their disagreement over the extent of the form and the structure, Putney and Booth together have done much to cause *Tristram Shandy* to be regarded as more than the result of an author's whim. They have also helped to cause Tristram's commentary to be taken seriously. Although Booth has disagreed with Putney, he has made the following comment about his article: "It is an excellent account of the first five and a half volumes, with perhaps the strongest praise for Sterne's structural gifts ever written." [16] And while Booth has contended for more form in *Tristram Shandy* than many readers would be willing to grant, he succeeded in increasing the general acceptance of some form for it.

Mid-twentieth-century criticism has made some progress in determining whether some of the contents of *Tristram Shandy* should have been included and whether more should have been written to complete it. With some reservations about the faultless state of the novel, it will be assumed in the present chapter that *Tristram Shandy* has a certain degree of recognizable form and completeness and that with few exceptions Sterne kept himself

[14] *Ibid.*, p. 163.
[15] "Did Sterne Complete *Tristram Shandy*?", p. 177.
[16] *Ibid.*

aloof from his work, generally wrote as a sure artist, and in many cases carried out his original intentions. The following parts of the novel that appear to have a place in the total structure will be surveyed: the part Uncle Toby plays in the life of Tristram Shandy up to the breeching of the hero; the war games which end with the Treaty of Utrecht; the Le Fever episode; the courtship of the Widow Wadman; the interruption of the courtship in which Tristram relates his European journey; the resumption of the courtship and its conclusion; and, finally, the conclusion of the book.

A sequence of events concerning Uncle Toby and Tristram appears to form one of the parts of the novel. H. K. Russell and Dorothy Van Ghent in commenting on Tristram's invocation to the "powers" for aid, neglected to mention that Tristram was concerned with what events he should relate in the different parts of the novel. Tristram evidently saw his work as one in which parts were important.

The story in one sense, is certainly out of its place here; for by right it should come in, either among the anecdotes of my uncle *Toby's* amours with the widow *Wadman*, in which Corporal *Trim* was no mean actor, or else in the middle of his and Corporal *Trim's* campaigns on the bowling green, – for it will do very well in either place; – but then if I reserve it for either of those parts of the story, – I ruin the story I'm upon, – and if I tell it here – I anticipate matters and ruin it.

O, ye Powers! (for powers ye are, and great ones too) – which enable mortal man to tell a story worth the hearing, – that kindly shew him, where he is to begin it, – and where he is to end it – what he is to put into it, – and what he is to leave out. . . .[17]

Tristram has been sufficiently explicit concerning Uncle Toby's campaigns and amours as parts of the novel for the reader to determine what story he is "upon now". He is, of course, telling the story of what happened in his prenatal existence. It has been argued in chapter five of this study that he is also telling the story of himself and his father. It is now proposed that Tristram is also telling the story of himself and his uncle, and that the latter over-

[17] *Tristram Shandy*, p. 207.

laps the story of himself and his father. That story begins in Volume I, Chapter III and ends in Volume VI, Chapter XIX; the part containing that of his father and himself begins in Volume I, Chapter I and ends in Volume IV, Chapter XIX.

The narrator begins the Tristram-Uncle Toby sequence by making his uncle responsible for the information concerning the begetting scene. After having related the circumstances attending his geniture, he begins Chapter III by writing: "To my uncle Mr. *Toby Shandy* do I stand indebted for the preceding anecdote, to whom my father had often complained of the injury."

A dozen short chapters later the narrator intimates that he learned from Uncle Toby of his parents' return from London after Elizabeth, the year before he was begotten, had been carried up to London "upon false cries and tokens" of pregnancy. "My mother, whatever was her journey up, had but an uneasy time of it down. – In a word, as she complained to my uncle Toby, he [Walter] would have tired out the patience of any flesh alive." [18]

By observing Uncle Toby, Tristram had been able to know something about himself. He studied his uncle's character:

There appeared many strong lines in it of a family likeness, which shewed that he derived the singularity of his temper ... from blood. ... And I have often wondered, that my father ... upon his observing some tokens of eccentricity in my course of behavior when I was a boy, – should never once endeavour to account for them in this way; for all of the SHANDY FAMILY were of an original character throughout; I mean the males.[19]

From his uncle, Tristram learned compassion, for he says in Volume II of the fly-loosing episode:

This I know that the lesson of universal good-will then taught and imprinted by my uncle *Toby*, has never been worn out of my mind ... I often think that I owe one half of my philanthropy to that one accidental impression.[20]

Moreover, Uncle Toby is given credit for all of the misfortunes that attended Tristram's birth. In the marriage contract between

---

[18] *Tristram Shandy*, p. 43.
[19] *Ibid.*, p. 65.
[20] *Ibid.*, p. 114.

Walter and Elizabeth Shandy a clause was inserted, which, says Tristram, "would never have been thought of at all but for my uncle Toby Shandy". The contract stated that as often as Elizabeth should happen to be with child, she should travel to London for her "delivery and lying-in".[21] The clause Uncle Toby added for the protection of his brother stipulated that in case Elizabeth put Walter to the "expense of a *London* journey upon false cries and tokens; that for every such instance she should forfeit all the right and title to which the covenant gave her to the next turn".[22] Elizabeth forfeited her right by going to London on a false alarm; and on the night of the begetting of Tristram, Walter informed her that she must lie in of this child in the country.[23] "I was doomed, says Tristram, to have my nose squeezed as flat to my face, as if the destinies had actually spun me without one." [24] He then promises to deal with this calamity in the following fashion:

> How this event came about, – and what a train of vexatious disappointments, in one stage or another of my life, have pursued me from the mere loss, or rather compression, of this single member, – shall be laid before the reader in due time.[25]

Booth has argued that "as for the troubles resulting from the flattened nose, we have certainly been given them aplenty by the end of Vol. IX". But it is much more obvious that Tristram relates "how this event came about". Uncle Toby has the clause put into the document; Walter insists on carrying it out; Elizabeth lies-in in the country; Walter Shandy gets Dr. Slop to stand by in case the midwife should fail; when she does fail, Dr. Slop takes over and breaks the child's nose in delivery. The breaking of Tristram's nose and the changing of his name from 'Trismegistus" to "Tristram", as it was pointed out in the previous chapter, marks the end of the Walter-Tristram sequence. When Walter in "My Father's Lamentation" enumerates the list of evils which had befallen his son, although neither he nor his brother appears to be

---

[21] *Ibid.*, pp. 38 f.
[22] *Ibid.*, p. 40.
[23] *Ibid.*, p. 43.
[24] *Ibid.*, p. 41.
[25] *Tristram Shandy*, p. 41.

conscious of the fact, he recites them to the very man who had been responsible.

But the Tristram-Toby sequence continues. Tristram also makes Uncle Toby responsible for the window-sash catastrophe which terminated the hero's infancy, and which he says was responsible for his condition in later life.[26] This event had its beginning in the early part of the novel. Although Tristram had been drawing the character of Uncle Toby ever since he had introduced him in Chapter III of Volume I, he announced in Chapter XXIII that he would draw his uncle's character from his hobby; for, said he, "doubtless, there is a communication between them of some kind", and "the HOBBY-HORSE which my uncle always rode upon is well worth giving a description of".[27] In the remainder of Volume I and in the beginning chapters of Volume II Tristram relates how and why Uncle Toby came by it. After having been wounded in the groin at the siege of Namur, he was returned to England. The healing of the wound was delayed when he "fretted and fumed inwardly" and brought "sharp exacerbations to his wound" by trying to describe the siege of Namur. " 'Twas not by ideas, – by heaven! his life was put in jeopardy by words." [28] Upon finding that a map of the city of Namur enabled him to make himself understood, he proceeded to study other maps. Led by a thirst for more knowledge, he read books on military architecture and the science of projectiles. He then took up the study of higher mathematics; but since the study of the conic section angered his groin, he stopped and turned back to the practical study of fortifications.[29]

For four years (1696-1700) he had read and studied about fortifications. When he turned to a practical study of them, his servant, Trim, suggested that the two of them go to Shandy Hall and there lay out fortified towns on the bowling greens.[30] But the

---

[26] Wayne C. Booth, "Did Sterne Complete *Tristram Shandy?*", p. 181, n. 18.
[27] *Tristram Shandy*, pp. 77 f.
[28] *Ibid.*, p. 87.
[29] *Ibid.*, p. 91.
[30] *Ibid.*, p. 97.

story of Uncle Toby and Trim and the war games must wait says Tristram:

> How my uncle *Toby* and Corporal *Trim* managed this matter, – with the history of their campaigns, which were no way barren of events, – may make no uninteresting underplot in the *epitasis* and working up of this drama. – At present the scene must drop, and change for the parlor fireside.[31]

The story does wait until Tristram, after invoking the powers, decides to tell a small part of it. But he delays the account of the war games until after the window falls and Susannah runs to Uncle Toby's house for sanctuary. Trim, believing that he too is culpable, consoles her. But Tristram makes Uncle Toby culpable:

> Uncle Toby has as much of the bloodshed to answer for the heaven as either of 'em; – so that neither reason or instinct, separate or together, could possibly have guided Susannah's steps to so proper an asylum. . . . 'Tis my own affair: I'll explain it myself.[32]

Tristram then devotes twelve pages to relating how the hobby horse had finally led to an extensive use of leaden cannons and how the confiscation of materials to make them had led to taking out the window-sash weight. Although it follows the catastrophe, the narration belongs to it.

The narrative also belongs to another part of the novel which begins at the conclusion of the breeching scene, where it can be recalled Rufus D. Putney found a change in the novel had taken place.[33] Tristram has been breeched and the narrator announces that he has entered upon a new scene of events. Trim and Uncle Toby are next displayed in their full enjoyment of firing toy cannons with puffs of tobacco smoke. Tristram now announces that this is enough. He will wheel off Uncle Toby's ordnance and "exhibit my uncle Toby dressed in a new character, throughout which the world can have no idea how he will act".[34]

Tristram wheels off the ordnance by having the Treaty of Utrecht and the demolition of Dunkirk bring an end to the war

---

[31] *Ibid.*, p. 99.
[32] *Ibid.*, pp. 376 f.
[33] See above, p. 132.
[34] *Tristram Shandy*, p. 455.

games and provide Uncle Toby leisure for courting the Widow Wadman. The story of the courtship, except for a major interruption in the telling, will continue almost to the end of *Tristram Shandy*.

The story of the affair had been promised more than once. In Volume I Tristram had promised to tell it in order to explain Captain Shandy's unusual silence in the presence of women.[35] In Volume II Uncle Toby had declared that the shock he "received a year after the demolition of *Dunkirk*", in his affair with the Widow Wadman, had given him "cause to say that he knew nothing about women, or their concerns either".[36]

But before the relevance of the courtship to the remainder of the novel can be investigated, the interruption of the story must be examined in some detail.

The relation of Tristram's European journey comprises all of Volume VII, and it has posed a problem for those who would see *Tristram Shandy* as a novel as well as for those who would regard it as autobiography.

When Wilbur Cross, who believed that the work was "in large part autobiographical",[37] came to discuss Volume VII, he insisted that the relation was that of Sterne's own journey, although he was forced to admit that the author here had "substituted Mr. Tristram Shandy for himself".[38]

One of the structural critics, D. W. Jefferson, has said that "the freakish episodes of Continental travel [are] unrelated to rest of the work".[39] Another, Rufus D. Putney, has dismissed the journey

---

[35] *Ibid.*, p. 67. Cf. H. K. Russell, "*Tristram Shandy* and the Technique of the Novel", *SP*, XLII (1945), p. 590. "The method of *Tristram Shandy* does not subordinate antecedent events to an arbitrary arrangement of calendar time; it integrates them with the portrayal of character, carefully leading the reader's train of ideas."
[36] *Life*, p. xiii.
[37] *Ibid.*, p. 101.
[38] *Ibid.*, pp. 354-355.
[39] "*Tristram Shandy* and its Tradition", in *From Dryden to Johnson: The Pelican Guide to English Literature* (Hormondsworth, Middlesex, Penguin Books, Ltd., 1957), IV, p. 339. [Jefferson's essay in the *Pelican Guide* was adapted from his article, "*Tristram Shandy* and the Tradition of Learned Wit", *EC*, I (1951), pp. 225-248.]

along with the affairs of Uncle Toby as an interpolation.[40] Wayne Booth would make it, as well as the affairs of Uncle Toby, a part of the entire structure, although he expends little effort in justifying the place of the journey in *Tristram Shandy*. "In the fourth installment (January, 1765), after the trip abroad in Volume VII, which fulfills his promise to go on with his own story, Volume VIII begins the affairs in earnest." [41]

In Volume VII a journey is related for which no promise has been made. John Croft, younger brother of Sterne's friend, Stephen Croft, wrote that the author "intended to travel his hero Tristram Shandy all over Europe . . . and at length to return Tristram well informed and a compleat English Gentleman".[42] When Tristram related the story of Uncle Toby and the fly, he gave credit to the impression of the action for half of his philanthropy; the other half was due to the "study of the *literae humaniores*, at the university and the helps of an expensive education bestowed upon [him], both at home and abroad".[43] But Tristram promises to relate a story of his grand tour only after he is well along in describing an entirely different kind of journey in Volume VII, and this promise was never fulfilled.

The promise of an entirely different kind of journey from that of Tristram's majority or from the one he related in Volume VII had been made in Volume I.

I had just had time in my journey through Denmark with Mr. Noddy's eldest son, whom in 1741, I accompanied as governor, riding along at a prodigious rate, throughout most of *Europe*, and of which journey, perform'd by us two a most delectable narrative will be given in the progress of this work.[44]

---

[40] "Laurence Sterne, Apostle of Laughter", p. 163.
[41] Wayne C. Booth, "Did Sterne Complete *Tristram Shandy?*", p. 180.
[42] Quoted by Work in *Tristram Shandy*, xvi.
[43] *Tristram Shandy*, p. 114.
[44] *Tristram Shandy*, p. 24. Wilbur Cross and Leslie Stephens believed that Sterne made the journey in 1741. See *Life*, p. 57, and "Laurence Sterne", in *DNB*, XVIII, p. 1089. Theodore Baird has commented on the puzzling nature of the passage: "There is little in Tristram's character as it is later revealed to suggest competence as a bear leader." See "The Time Scheme of *Tristram Shandy*", *PMLA*, LI (1936), p. 818.

But nothing more is ever said by Tristram about the "delectable narrative". Between Volumes I and VII no more promises are made to write about any kind of journey, although the set of circumstances related in the fourth volume could lead to his making the kind of tour he had mentioned in the fly-loosing episode. After the misnaming of Tristram, Walter "is rescued out of his indecision whether to lay out the legacy of one thousand pounds he has received from Aunt Dinah" to send his eldest son, Bobby, abroad. Bobby dies. "From this moment", writes Tristram, "I am to be considered the heir apparent to the Shandy family." [45] But what decision Walter makes about sending Tristram abroad is not then revealed.

That Walter actually had decided to send his heir on the journey is related in Volume VII, in which the hero, far past the time for completing his education by a trip abroad, is describing a different kind of journey, a flight from death.

Volume VII must be examined closely before it can be seen as a part of *Tristram Shandy*, for it does indeed appear to be autobiographical and to have little connection with the remainder of the work. Sterne himself five years before writing it had interrupted his own writing to make a tour of Europe.

Over exertion had brought on the most severe hemorrhage Sterne had ever had.... For some time he had been thinking about going abroad.... His severe illness now settled the matter for him.... Towards the second week in January [1762], Sterne started across the channel in a race with death.[46]

Fredman declares that "Book VII of *Tristram Shandy* . . . could not have been written if Sterne had not traveled abroad." [47] A threat of death to Sterne was the same kind of threat to Tristram. Cross, some years ago, and Fredman, more recently, have found little structural relevance of this part of the book to the remainder of it. Cross called it a case of grafting: "Notes he had made for the journey, but it had not occurred to him that they could be grafted into *Tristram Shandy*. They were to form as first designed,

---

[45] *Tristram Shandy*, p. 336.
[46] *Life*, p. 288.
[47] *Diderot and Sterne*, p. 128.

a work separate and apart." [48] And Fredman's comment has something less than praise for the artistry: "Sterne had become desperate for both money and materials for his book, so he hit on the idea of making over some of his travel notes into a comic tour of France for Volume VII." [49]

Shaw, however, has regarded the travels as part of the whole novel:

> For some years more the reader of *Tristram Shandy* will still be expected to wander into the kitchen or parlour, bedroom or bowling green, or across the Channel throughout the towns and highways of France, exactly as the hobby horse pleases; the author will be just as ready to ramble off into the "nice and ticklish" discussions as in the earlier volumes.[50]

Sterne through Tristram has not been idle in defending the place the journey occupies in the work. In Volume I Tristram had written:

> You see, I have constructed the main work and the adventitious parts of it with such intersections, and have so complicated and involved the digressive and progressive movements, one with another, that the whole machine has been kept a going; — and what's more, It shall be kept a going these forty years, if it pleases the fountain of good health to bless me so long with life and good spirits.[51]

After Tristram, or Sterne — it is hard to say whether Sterne or Tristram should be considered responsible — has declared in the epigraph to Volume VII that "this is not an excursion from it, but the work itself",[52] Tristram begins the first chapter by calling attention to a qualifying clause he had inserted in his original declaration of intentions:

> No — I think, I said, I would write two volumes every year.... I swore it should be kept a going these forty years if it pleased but the fountain of life to bless so long with health and good spirits.[53]

Although he has been given a sufficient amount of good spirits to enable him to jest with death, he has not been given enough

[48] *Life*, p. 330.
[49] *Diderot and Sterne*, p. 159.
[50] *The Making of a Humorist*, p. 270.
[51] *Tristram Shandy*, p. 37.
[52] *Ibid.*, p. 477.
[53] *Tristram Shandy*, p. 479. See also pp. 73 f.

good health to prevent death from threatening him. In fact, death has entered and has seized him by the throat. He cannot think of writing now; he must, if he can, get away from death.

Had I not better, *Eugenius*, fly for my life? 'Tis my advice, my dear *Tristram*, said *Eugenius* – then by heaven! I will lead him a dance he little thinks of – for I will gallop, quoth I, without looking behind me to the banks of the *Garonne*; and if I hear him clattering at my heels – I'll scamper away to mount *Vesuvius*.... *Allons!* said I. The post boy gave a crack to his whip – off I went like a cannon, and in half a dozen bounds got into *Dover*.[54]

A brief review of the way Tristram gives an account of his journey should reveal something of the way Volume VII is related to the remainder of the novel.

The precipitate flight does not allow him time to stop a moment to give the character of the people, or to look at the cities. "It was dusky in the evening when I landed [at Calais], and dark as pitch in the morning when I set out." [55] At Boulogne greater haste is needed: "I'm pursued myself like a hundred devils, and shall be overtaken before I can change horses... Do stop that death-looking, long-striding scare sinner who is posting after me." [56] At Montrueil, he fears that death might be nearer than he had imagined.[57] He has scarcely time to see more of Paris than "that the streets are nasty".[58] Tristram advises the reader to "read his free translation of the inscription upon the portico of the Louvre".

Earth no such folks! – no folks e'er such a town as Paris is! – Sing, derry, derry, down.[59]

Finally, however, he is able to outdistance his pursuer:

"I have followed many a man thro' France", quoth he – "but never at this mettlesome rate". Still he followed, – and still I fled him – but I fled him cheerfully – still he pursued – but like one who pursued his prey without hope – as he lagg'd every step he lost softened his looks – why should I fly him at this rate? [60]

[54] See also *Letters*, p. 377, for a similar statement by Sterne.
[55] *Tristram Shandy*, p. 483.
[56] *Ibid.*, p. 487.
[57] *Ibid.*, p. 491.
[58] *Ibid.*, p. 498.
[59] *Ibid.*, p. 501.
[60] *Ibid.*, p. 534.

"He danced all the way", Cross has said, "from Lunel to Montpellier, and thence on through Narbonne and Carcassone to his habitation at Toulouse [on the banks of the Garonne]." [61]

Safe in Toulouse, Tristram writes about the journey from the notes he had made en route. And, after he has completed the account, he resumes writing about his uncle's love affair. "Pulling a paper of black lines, that I might go straightforward, without digression or parenthesis, in my *uncle* Toby's amours – I begun thus –." [62]

The account of the journey has been anything but a morbid one. He has jested about his narrow escapes from the "long-striding scare sinner", and he has included some other material which is "laugh-at-able in its own way".[63] He tells the story of feeding an ass a macaroon and getting his breeches torn in return;[64] and he relates another story in which his feelings of sympathy are made ridiculous – he finds the tomb of two lovers is no longer there when he goes to drop tears upon it.[65] Although he wonders if he should have done so, he includes the story of the Abbess of Andouillets and the little novitiate.[66] But he does not need to defend the description of his taking part in a village dance and of his dancing his way across southern France.[67]

He has also included the story of losing and recovering the notes he has been making en route. "The chaise vamper's wife took them from her curls and put them gravely one by one into my hat . . . and when they are published they will be worse twisted still." [68] And he does indeed succeed in getting time hopelessly entangled when he described how he is writing the account from the notes:

I have brought myself into such a situation as no traveller ever stood before me, for I am at this moment walking across the market place

[61] *Life*, p. 327.
[62] *Tristram Shandy*, p. 476.
[63] *Letters*, p. 74.
[64] Cf. *Life*, p. 322. Cross calls it "The famous communion with the ass at Lyons".
[65] *Tristram Shandy*, p. 526.
[66] *Ibid.*, p. 503.
[67] *Ibid.*, p. 525.
[68] *Ibid.*, p. 528.

at Auxerre ... and I am at this moment entering Lyons [where the accident to the notes occurred] ... and I am moreover this moment in a handsome pavillion ... upon the banks of the Garonne ... where I now sit rhapsodizing these affairs – Let me recollect myself and pursue my journey.[69]

At Auxerre, Tristram recalls an incident which had occurred there on his previous journey, and he reveals that he had actually made the grand tour:

But for Auxerre – (I could go on forever; for in my *grand tour* through *Europe*, in which, after all, my father (not caring to trust me with anyone) attended me himself, with my uncle *Toby*, and *Trim*, and *Obadiah*, and indeed most of the family except my mother....[70]

Furthermore, an account of the grand tour will form a part of *Tristram Shandy*. Tristram says that when the story of that journey has been written it will be different from any tour of Europe which was ever executed. "The fault must be mine and mine only – if it be not read by all travellers and travel readers, till travelling is no more." But, "this rich bale is not to be opened now except a small thread or two of it, merely to unravel the mystery of my father's stay at Auxerre".[71]

The small thread he unravels displays the Shandy characters, talking and acting as they do in the other parts of *Tristram Shandy*. But it is all that he ever shows of the bale, for the full story of the grand tour was never written.

The journey described at length in Volume VII obviously should not be confused with any other the author has promised or prepared for. Moreover, it is presented as an unexpected interruption. But, interruption though it is, in it Tristram Shandy appears more than he does in any other part of the novel. As the epigraph to Volume VII states, "This is not an excursion from it, but the work itself."

Since the beginning of the novel in 1759, Tristram, a writer in his forties, had been relating events which occurred before and up to his fifth year, 1723. After the breeching scene in Volume

[69] *Ibid.*, pp. 515-516.
[70] *Ibid.*, p. 514.
[71] *Ibid.*, p. 514.

VI, he went back to relate events which had taken place five years before his geniture and birth. Before Volume VII Tristram had been the narrator and the events had some connection with his life and opinions, but in much of that part young Tristram did not appear on the scene. But in the journey Tristram relates events in which he, not long before, had been the principal actor.

But Tristram does not end the novel with his having found, for a time, security against death. In the eighth volume he resumes the story of Uncle Toby and the events which took place in the nine months between the demolition of Dunkirk and the shock the Captain received at the conclusion of the courtship. In Volume IX he will reveal the nature of the shock. After he reveals it, only two short chapters will remain, and *Tristram Shandy* will be ended.

Wayne Booth, who contends for nearly complete structure, has seen that Sterne brought the novel to completion in the last two chapters of Volume IX.[72] Although Alice Green Fredman, who is more concerned with effect than with structure *per se*, has recognized that Sterne concluded *Tristram Shandy* in the last two chapters, she has seen the ending of an interesting part of it in the final revelation of what had shocked Uncle Toby:

> At last shortly before the conclusion of the novel, he explains what caused Captain Shandy's innocent amazement which he mentions early in Book II. It had taken him, intermittently, eight volumes to come to the heart of the matter, and the denouément should be no surprise to the audience, but by assorted digressions, Sterne has managed to imbue it with enough fire so that the reader is left curious to learn Uncle Toby's reactions.[73]

It is hard to relate the account of Uncle Toby's love affair to the life and opinions of Tristram Shandy. Nowhere does Tristram say that the amours affected himself. On the other hand, the story of what happened to Uncle Toby could be seen as a part of the novel if it were regarded as an exhibition of the story-telling power Tristram has learned to exercise. One might reasonably do so, for

---

[72] "Did Sterne Complete *Tristram Shandy*?", p. 181.
[73] *Diderot and Sterne*, p. 144.

a good part of the life of the hero has been presented to the reader as that of Tristram the writer.

In Volume VIII Tristram by emphasizing his role of writer establishes a continuity between the journey he has recently taken and the affairs of Uncle Toby which had taken place before the writer was born. Although the place in which he has found safety does permit him to go on with the story, it is not conducive to serious writing. "In these sportive plains and under this genial sun ... the judgment is surprised by the imagination." [74] He then shows how his manner of writing is being affected: "I begin with writing the first sentence – and trusting to Almighty God for the second." [75] Evidently, his trust has not been misplaced. Despite his carelessness, he is moving toward his subject. He will write for the most hypocritical of readers; he asks about the health of the hypocrite's family; he is reminded of his own health and the medical treatment he has been receiving. It is useless, he swears by the first thing which crosses his mind, which happens to be his Great Aunt Dinah's velvet mask. From Aunt Dinah's mask it is only a short step to Uncle Toby's not being able to bear the name of Aunt Dinah mentioned. Tristram can now begin to tell the story of Uncle Toby's unfortunate affair with the concupiscent widow, which had been responsible for the Captain's aversion to hearing about his amatory relative, Aunt Dinah.

Tristram then proceeds to tell everything about the love affair, from its incipience to the beginning of Uncle Toby's active part in it. Lacking a bed when he first came down to Shandy Hall, Uncle Toby had accepted one from the Widow Wadman, whose house adjoined his bowling green. The widow then had fallen in love with the captain, but not until eleven years later did he learn that he and the widow loved each other. After the Treaty of Utrecht had made his war games useless, after two attacks by her, and after a blister close to his groin has burst, he knows he is in love and decides to go courting her. Volume VIII ends with his and Trim's preparation to besiege the Widow Wadman.

The story of the siege and its termination had to wait until the

---
[74] *Tristram Shandy*, p. 539.
[75] *Ibid.*, p. 540.

next, and the last, installment, which contained only one volume, Volume IX. Cross believed that Sterne had intended to write and include a tenth volume, because on January 6, 1767, before the installment appeared on the 30th, Sterne had written: "I miscarried of my tenth volume through the violence of a fever." [76]

In the ninth volume there are indications, however, that the work, or at least the story of Uncle Toby, is being brought to a close. In one place Tristram laments to "Dear Jenny" that "time wastes too fast: every letter I trace tells me with what rapidity Life follows my pen. Every time I kiss thy hand to bid adieu, and every absence which follows it, are preludes to that eternal separation which we are shortly to make." [77] In another he indicates that he is losing interest in telling the story of Uncle Toby's affair:

Let us drop the metaphor – and the story too – if you please: for though I have all this time been hastening toward this part with so much earnest desire, as well as knowing it to be the choicest morsel of which I had to offer the world, yet now that I am got to it, any one is welcome to take by pen, and go on with the story that will – [78]

This remark of Tristram's might be disregarded if Sterne by this time had not been the sick man he was, he died the following year.[79] A few pages later Sterne practically drops the mask to speak in his own right:

It is one comfort to me, that I lost some fourscore ounces of blood this week in a most uncritical fever which attacked at the beginning of this chapter; so that I still have some hopes remaining, it may be more in the serous or globular part of the blood, than in the subtile *aura* of the brain.[80]

As William Bowen Piper has remarked recently, "In Volume IX death catches up with Tristram at last." [81]

Although Sterne in his dedication of Volume IX called the volume "the Amours of Uncle Toby",[82] he gives several indica-

[76] *Life*, p. 422.
[77] *Tristram Shandy*, p. 611.
[78] *Tristram Shandy*, p. 627.
[79] *Life*, p. 486.
[80] *Tristram Shandy*, p. 627.
[81] "Tristram Shandy's Tragicomical Testimony", *Criticism*, III (Summer, 1961), p. 183.
[82] *Tristram Shandy*, p. 597.

THE NOVEL: TO THE FINAL COMMENT OF YORICK 149

tions that he is also winding up the affairs of Tristram. Booth has contended that Sterne gathered up nearly all of the threads of the story in the final volume.[83] One can readily find several connections in it with the previous volumes like that of the recurrence of the address to "Dear, Dear Jenny", which Cross has noticed.[84] Tristram's parents walked arm in arm "till they got to the fatal angle of the old garden wall, where [in Volume II] Doctor *Slop* was overthrown by Obadiah on the coach horse".[85] They were also "reminded by Yorick's congregation coming out of the church"[86] that it was the first Sunday in the month, a date of great importance in the first volume. While he is explaining the widow's curiosity,[87] Tristram recalls the Tale of Slawkenbergius, which he had recounted in Volume IV. And once while pondering how he could tell the story, Tristram recalls that when he was journeying across France [in Volume VII], the thoughts of Uncle Toby's amours had harmonized his feelings with those of the beautiful, wandering girl, Maria, who was demented because her marriage banns had been forbidden. He reminds himself that then the jester in him had caused him to "let fall an unseasonable pleasantry in the venerable presence of misery".[88]

The story of the courtship is a simple one. Captain Shandy marches into the Mrs. Wadman's house, announces that he is in love, and settles down for her to accept him. Nine months later he is still waiting for her answer. In the meantime she has been trying to find out if his wound has not unfitted him for what she wants in a husband. She asks him a thousand questions about his wound, and he tells her everything about it except what she wants to know. Her maid, Bridgett, directly questions Trim, who assures Bridgett that his master had not been emasculated. Bridgett gives Trim, along with other benefits, "the secret articles which delayed the whole surrender". He then informs his master why the widow has been so curious about the wound. Uncle Toby, who

[83] "Did Sterne Complete *Tristram Shandy?*", p. 175.
[84] *Life*, p. 425.
[85] *Tristram Shandy*, p. 611.
[86] *Ibid.*, p. 614.
[87] *Ibid.*, pp. 624 f.
[88] *Ibid.*, pp. 628-631.

has believed her questions were motivated by compassion, is now through with love and women.

Sterne gives almost as much emphasis to the interest others take in the affair as to the romance itself. That of Tristram's parents comprises the first chapter, a part of the second, and all of the tenth and the eleventh. Mrs. Shandy's lack of interest in the cause of the delay, the peculiar interest the servants take in it, and the townspeople's curiosity about it are related in the beginning of the next to the last chapter:

> Mrs. *Bridget*, who had a secret of her own to carry, had got happily delivered of both to Susannah behind the garden wall. As for my mother, she saw nothing in it, to make the least bustle about – but *Susannah* was sufficient by herself for all the ends and purposes you could possibly have in exporting a family secret; for she instantly imported it by signs to Jonathan – and *Jonathan* by tokens to the cook.... The cook sold it with some kitchen-fat to the postillion for a groat, who trucked it with the dairy maid for something about the same value.... Not an old woman in the village or five miles round who did not understand the difficulties of my uncle Toby's siege, and what were the secret articles which delayed his whole surrender.[89]

But, with Uncle Toby's discovery of what had delayed the surrender, Tristram ended the story towards which he had all along been hastening with so much earnest desire, as well knowing it to be the choicest morsel of what [he] had to offer to the world.[90] The two remaining chapters are taken up largely with the opinions that the people of the Shandy world held about the affair.

In the beginning chapters of Volume IX, Walter Shandy had been forced to conclude that his wife, lacking "the least mote or speck of desire",[91] was interested in the courtship only insofar as it might end in marriage and children. In the concluding chapters Elizabeth Shandy sees nothing in the widow's curiosity "to make the least bustle about": [92] in a case as doubtful as that of Uncle Toby any woman would want to make sure that the suitor was able to beget children.

[89] *Ibid.*, pp. 643 f.
[90] *Ibid.*, p. 627.
[91] *Ibid.*, pp. 599 f.
[92] *Ibid.*, p. 643.

After Sterne has presented the way the servants and the world regarded the reason for the widow's delay, he shows the different views the Shandies and the minister, Yorick, take of it. Uncle Toby, terribly hurt, is coming to his brother for consolation. Elizabeth is, of course, indifferent. Elizabeth, Dr. Slop, and Yorick, present when Walter learns of the trespass done his brother by the widow and by the world, hear him angrily declare "that the whole affair was lust". Prone to crucify truth by making hypotheses, Walter adds that all of the evils and disorders in the world have been caused by lust. How Yorick does so is not revealed, but he brings Walter's hypothesis "to some kind of temper". Uncle Toby, fallen from innocence but already bearing the "marks of infinite benevolence and forgiveness in his looks", then enters the room, and Walter breaks out anew.

In Volume V Tristram had said of one of Walter's speeches: "Yorick listened to my father with great attention; there was a seasoning of wisdom unaccountably mixed up with his strongest whims, and he sometimes had such illuminations in the darkest of his eclipses as almost atoned for them." [93]

What Tristram's father has to say now deserves close study, for it is not unrelated to what Tristram has been writing about since the beginning of the novel. Walter maintains that although the act of procreation is necessary, it is nonetheless shameful. He will not accept the view "that in itself, and simply taken – like hunger or thirst, or sleep – 'tis an affair neither good or bad, or shameful or otherwise." If it is not shameful, he asks, why is it done in secret? "Why is it so held as to be conveyed to a cleanly mind by no language, translation, or periphrasis?" It must be more shameful than war, for the latter and all that pertains to it is not only mentioned freely but glorified. Yorick is rising up to batter the whole hypothesis to pieces – the reader is never told how –, when Obadiah bursts in to the room with a complaint which causes Walter to modify his conclusions about the way the procreative act is regarded.

Obadiah lodges a complaint against the Shandy bull to the man who is responsible for keeping the town bull. On the same day he

[93] *Tristram Shandy*, p. 404.

had married, Obadiah had taken his cow on a "pop visit". In due time Obadiah's wife had given birth to a child but the cow had not calved, and the townspeople have agreed with Obadiah that the bull is at fault. Walter had approved of the bull for going about his business with a grave face. The squire "knew that the world judged by events",[94] and he would now be glad, despite what he had been saying about the shameful way in which potency was regarded, if he could defend his bull's prowess.

Obadiah and Walter have overlooked the fact that the parish had been too large for the animal. Walter turns to Dr. Slop for help in shifting the blame to Obadiah's cow, but the doctor says that cows are never barren, although Obadiah's wife might have come before her time. "Prithee, has the child hair upon its head?" "It is as hairy as I am: said *Obadiah*. *Obadiah* had not been shaved for three weeks." Outrageous as the statement is, Obadiah has carried his point. Walter now turns to and addresses his brother, who has been suspected to being impotent, and before he concludes he directly addresses him again as if the words are peculiarly applicable to his case.

When – cried my father; beginning the sentence with an exclamatory whistle – and so, brother *Toby*, this poor Bull of mine, who is as good a BULL as ever p-ss'd, and might have done for *Europa* herself in purer times – had he but two leggs less, might have been driven into Doctor's Commons and lost his character – which to a Town Bull, brother *Toby*, is the very same thing as his life.

Although Walter's metaphor shifts back and forth from bull to man, he evidently is telling Uncle Toby that he might have been disgraced if he had married the widow: much would have been required of him, and if he had been unable to perform, the world would have learned about it.

The novel is now over except for a question asked by Mrs. Shandy, who could never grasp an implication, and an answer made by Yorick, whom Tristram has permitted to have the final words in the book. According to Jefferson, Tristram has told all.[95]

---

[94] *Ibid.*, p. 42.
[95] D. W. Jefferson, "*Tristram Shandy* and the Tradition of Learned Wit", *Essays in Criticism*, I (1951), p. 239 f.

Certain inferences can now be drawn concerning the meaning of the three final speeches in the novel. Sterne had reason to be concerned about the reception of the ninth volume: it contained as many daring items as, if not more than, the previous installments. Besides the indecent curiosity of the Widow Wadman, there were Trim's story of Tom and the Jew's widow, Trim's affair with Bridgett, the servant's handling of the secret, and Obadiah's complaint against the Shandy bull. If Sterne intended for the ninth volume to complete the work, all of *Tristram Shandy*, of which the last volume formed a part, was ready for judgment. That Sterne showed a concern for the judgment of later generations may be seen in Chapter VII of Volume IX. What he has written "shall be thumbed over by Posterity ... I say by Posterity – and care not, if I repeat the word again for what has this book done more than the Legation of Moses or the Tale of a Tub, that it may not swim down the gutter of Time along with them." [96] It should be noticed that he has compared his work with those of two other clergymen.

Since the life of Tristram Shandy began five years after Uncle Toby's courtship ended, the characters and the situations in the last scene in the book should not be what they are because of anything that has happened in the first five and a half volumes. But they are the creations of Tristram, who was developed in the first part of the book. The life of the hero was a relation of not only how he came to be what he was but how he was experimenting with writing. In a great many cases he has wondered how successfully he has been carrying on the writing. There is, however, in the last volumes less of worrying about the kind of writing he is doing than there is about his continuing to have enough life and spirit to complete the writing.

"My way is ever to point out to the curious, different tracts of investigations, to come at the first springs of the events I tell," [97] Tristram had written in the beginning of the work and after he had made a short digression. At the end of this long digression

---

[96] *Tristram Shandy*, p. 610.
[97] *Tristram Shandy*, p. 66.

from the life of Tristram Shandy to relate the amours of Uncle Toby, some of the springs of the events he had first related should now be evident. The final speech of Walter can be made to take on meaning when it is regarded as a possible spring of the events Tristram has related in the beginning Volumes. It can be recalled that in the first volume Walter was very much concerned about "the condolences of his friends, and the foolish figure they should both make in church" after Mrs. Shandy had carried him up to London upon false cries and tokens "of being ready to lie in".[98] It can also be recalled that at the end of Tristram's infancy rumor had it that the falling window had castrated the child.[99] Walter thereupon decided to put him into breeches. Walter's regard for the way the world looked at the matter caused him to put the child into breeches. In the final scene in the book Walter has been made very much aware of the way the world has looked upon his bull and his brother. Potency in the eyes of the world is as dear as life itself.

According to Ernest Bernbaum, Sterne "wished to relate not so much what his characters did, but precisely what, when things happened to them, their mental and emotional reactions were".[100] In the last part of the book things are happening around instead of to Tristram's mother. Elizabeth Shandy, who had asked the "unseasonable question" at the beginning of the novel, in the last volume of the work wonders if Uncle Toby's love affair will lead to marriage and children. Devoid of pruriency, she cannot understand Mrs. Wadman's kind of interest in Uncle Toby.

After the conclusion of the courtship and in the final chapter of the book, Mrs. Shandy, who has already been presented as unable to understand a simple implication, is puzzled, of course, by her husband's speech that has baffled people far more acute than she is. And if Walter has been showing the high regard men have for potency, she has even more reason for her lack of understanding. Two words, "all" and "story", in her query make it un-

---

[98] *Ibid.*, p. 42.
[99] *Ibid.*, p. 433.
[100] *Guide Through the Romantic Movement*, 2d ed. (New York, Ronald Press, 1949), p. 15.

THE NOVEL: TO THE FINAL COMMENT OF YORICK   155

certain, however, what she is asking about. "L...d! said my mother, what is *all* this story about?" [italics mine]. Walter can scarcely be said to have told a story. The courtship that has been terminated could be called a story, but since she uses the word "all" and since her question comes at the end of the book, the reader has some reason for believing that Sterne has had Elizabeth ask what all "The Life and Opinions of Tristram Shandy, Gentleman" is about.

"A COCK and a BULL, said *Yorick* – And one of the best of its kind, I ever heard." Dorothy Van Ghent and B. H. Lehman have seen the answer to Elizabeth's question as being a bawdy joke.[101] Admittedly, the words written in capital letters afford a good reason for the view, and Walter's speech can be described by this kind of reading. There is, however, another part of the statement which makes the comment carry another meaning as well as the bawdy one; a cock-and-bull story is "a long idle rambling story; or a concocted, incredible story".[102] Yorick's saying it is one of the best of its kind he ever heard makes it appear that the second meaning is intended. Walter's speech is neither a long idle rambling nor a concocted, incredible one. If Sterne desired to conclude his work with a modest appraisal, the story of Uncle Toby's courtship and its conclusion with the affair of the Shandy bull might be described by Yorick's statement with its double meaning, but so can the entire work of *Tristram Shandy*. And since the statement ends the work there is even more reason to believe that Sterne has had Yorick pass judgment on the entire novel.

Yorick, after having been duly buried and lamented, was returned to the novel in Volume IV to arrange the Visitation Day dinner to decide whether or not the name of Tristram could be changed. He has made numerous appearances in Volumes V and

---

[101] Dorothy Van Ghent, *The English Novel: Form and Function*, p. 337; B. H. Lehman, "Of Time, Personality, and the Author", in *Studies in the Comic*, p. 284.
[102] Booth has made a good case for Sterne's being aware of this meaning of cock-and-bull story. See "Did Sterne Complete *Tristram Shandy*?", p. 181.

VI. He is nowhere about in Volume VII and appears only a time or two in Volume VIII. Aside from the mention of his "congregation coming out of church", which reminds Walter and Mrs. Shandy that it is the first Sunday in the month, he does not appear in the last volume before the last two chapters of it. There, he brings one of Walter's hypothesis to some temper, rises up to batter the whole of another to pieces, and then makes the last statement in the book.

One can notice that ever since Yorick has been returned he has been passing judgment on various matters – theology, warfare, political science, medicine, education, love, and procreation.[103] Almost invariably Tristram has permitted Yorick to have the final say. At the visitation dinner Yorick declares what preaching should be. In another case he passes judgment on Ecclesiastical wrangling and civil warfare by telling the story of Tripet and Gymnast. He declares while preaching the funeral sermon for Le Fever that "so soft and gentle a creature as man is was not shaped for" war. He takes the side of John Locke against Sir Robert Filmer on the question of hereditary monarchy when he congratulates Trim for his interpretation of the fifth commandment: Honor thy father and thy mother.[104] He makes Dr. Slop understand what he thinks about the teaching and the practice of medicine. And he gives his opinion about education: tutors should be "gentle tempered, generous and good".[105] Although he is interested in Walter's plan for increasing the understanding by the use of the auxiliary verbs, he shows that there is no way to increase man's intellectual ability.[106] At the beginning of Uncle Toby's courtship, he sees no reason for trying to divide love into two kinds, spiritual and carnal.[107] And for procreation, he finds it

---

[103] See *Tristram Shandy*, pp. 317, 386, 389, 393, 400, 401, 409, 415, 468, 586.
[104] See Wilfred Watson's contention for Yorick's political view and the importance of Trim's answer, in "The Fifth Commandment: Some Allusions to Sir Robert Filmer's Writings in *Tristram Shandy*", *MLN*, LXII (1947), pp. 234-240.
[105] *Tristram Shandy*, pp. 393, 400.
[106] *Ibid.*, p. 415.
[107] *Ibid.*, p. 468.

THE NOVEL: TO THE FINAL COMMENT OF YORICK 157

to be as important and matter of fact a subject to be dealt with as anything the reasoning faculty could produce.[108]

Yorick, who has been given the final say about many other matters, is the proper one to pass judgment on Tristram's experiment in writing a novel. Tristram has dealt with a subject which the words COCK and BULL could easily describe. On the other hand, an author's modest opinion of what he had accomplished could scarcely have been better than Yorick's comment. Albert Cook has said recently: "The fiction ends by reflexively calling itself a make believe cock and bull." [109] The fittingness of Yorick as the final judge can be seen in B. H. Lehman's description of him: "not one who blows the bubble of aspiration, but the descendant of the jester, whose function is to discourage delusions in mortals by pricking that bubble".[110]

Yorick was also a minister as Sterne himself had long been and still was. Traugott has said that "Sterne would have had to be even odder than he was, could he have forgotten so suddenly the habit of his office of preacher".[111] Sterne had published between the first and the last volumes of *Tristram Shandy* four volumes of the *Sermons of Mr. Yorick*. Two of the sermons, entitled "Pride", and "Humility", set forth the futility of all of man's efforts; another, "Search the Scriptures", declared the imaginative creations of man to be of little value.[112] Paul Stapfer in 1870, Wilbur Cross in 1929, Lansing Van der Hammond in 1948, and Rufus D. Putney in 1949, were in agreement that in his sermons Sterne "understood what he was saying and believed it".[113] Instead of marring his product Sterne's religious convictions would have helped establish in *Tristram Shandy* what Coleridge found praiseworthy:

---

[108] *Ibid.*, p. 586.
[109] "Reflexive Attitudes: Sterne, Gogol, Gide", *Criticism*, II (Summer, 1960), p. 169.
[110] "Of Time, Personality, and the Author", p. 248.
[111] *Tristram Shandy's World*, p. 150.
[112] *Sermons*, II, pp. 29-40, 41, 52, and 226-236.
[113] See *Laurence Sterne's Sermons of Mr. Yorick*, p. 97, for Van der Hammond's statement and his citing Stapfer and Cross. See Herbert Read's "Sterne" in *Sense of Glory* for one of the strongest contentions for Sterne's seriousness.

"The little is made great, and the great little, in order to destroy both; because all is equal in contrast with the infinite." [114]

The ninth volume terminated the writing career of Tristram. Although Sterne had one more year to write, in which time he could have continued *Tristram Shandy*, he turned instead to writing a series of letters to Mrs. Draper, the *Journal to Eliza* ("wrote under the fictitious names of Yorick to Eliza").[115] What was more important, he also began and wrote two volumes of *A Sentimental Journey* with Yorick as the narrator-hero of it. They were published in February before Sterne died on March 18, 1768.[116]

According to Richard Griffith, who had met him at Scarborough in September, 1767, Sterne had vowed then to "write no more Tristrams" but "to stick to Yorick".[117] "As nearly as can be determined", writes Rufus D. Putney, "Sterne conceived *A Sentimental Journey* during the summer of 1766 while he was busy with the last volume of *Tristram Shandy*." [118] Yorick's appearing at the last of the first novel was a fitting way of preparing the reader for the second one.

Yorick, who in the first volume of *Tristram Shandy* died because he had not been willing to explain his own actions, had been, in later volumes of the work, returned to explain a great many things, and in the last volume to make the final judgment. Although some subtle changes were made in his character to fit him for his new role, he would appear in another novel.

In the *Sentimental Journey* Yorick will not, as Tristram had done in the longer work, explain how he has come to be the per-

---

[114] Raysor (ed.), *Coleridge's Miscellaneous Criticism*, p. 444. For examples of the high regard in which Coleridge's statement is held see: John Traugott, *Tristram Shandy's World*, p. 72; Herbert Read, *Sense of Glory*, pp. 72 f.; Dorothy Van Ghent, *The English Novel: Form and Function*, p. 94; and Albert Cook, "Reflexive Attitudes, Sterne, Gogol, Gide", *Criticism*, II (1960), p. 165 f.
[115] *Life*, p. 440; *Work*, in *Tristram Shandy*, p. xli, agrees with Cross that the *Journal to Eliza* was written more as a preliminary to the *Sentimental Journey* than as something to be published.
[116] *Life*, pp. 477, 486.
[117] J. M. S. Tomkins, "Triglyph and Tristram", *TLS* (July 11, 1929).
[118] "Apostle of Laughter", *The Age of Johnson*, p. 167.

son and the writer he is, nor will he present the work as an experiment in writing. He will present himself as he is, and in many cases he will be like Sterne himself. And what he is will be revealed by the situations he will encounter. There will be a series of revelations of his feelings, the secret springs within himself, or as he calls them his "sentiments".

There will be no questions raised about the skill of the writer or the value of the literary product. That question had been answered in *Tristram Shandy*. It will be, as Cross and Work have agreed, and few have denied, "art so exquisite as to place the author among the first masters of English prose".[119] Although *Tristram Shandy* should, and probably would, have won Sterne a place among the great novelists, with a second which had been made possible by the first, his place was made doubly secure.

It was to *Tristram Shandy* that Sterne was chiefly indebted. Before he began writing it, his life in certain respects had been a failure. Not only had he acquired far less wealth and distinction than befitted a Sterne, but he had quarreled with his uncle, Jacques Sterne, the wealthy church politician, who could have helped his nephew to rich livings and ecclesiastical preferment. He had also by marrying Elizabeth Lumley failed to secure wealth or happiness. His literary achievements must have compensated in part for the failures.

Although *Tristram Shandy* was not altogether responsible for Sterne's comfort after 1759, it contributed greatly to it. How much Sterne's being lionized in London affected his receiving the rich living of Coxwold is uncertain.[120] But with the addition of the first two volumes of the *Sermons*, worth 140 pounds a year, and the purse of guineas given him by Bishop Warburton, Sterne received from his writing between eight and nine hundred pounds in 1760.[121] In that year at least, *Tristram Shandy* brought its author an income equal to that of Jacques Sterne.

And, of course, *Tristram Shandy* enabled Laurence Sterne to feel that he had "made his mark in the world". Lionized by the

---

[119] *Life*, p. 460; *Tristram Shandy*, p. xli.
[120] *This is Lorence*, p. 104.
[121] *Letters*, p. 203; *Four Portraits*, p. 156; *Life*, p. 224.

literary great in London, given a purse of guineas by Pope's literary executor, welcomed by Lord Bathurst (the friend of Swift and of Pope), and invited to Windsor – evidently here was Laurence's compensation for having been the poor relation of a distinguished family.

Finally, there is the matter of church preferment. Hartley says that *Tristram Shandy* began out of Sterne's despair over failing to gain church preferment.[122] How much preferment Sterne desired is unknown. If he wished to equal that of his great-grandfather, nothing less than that of archbishop would have satisfied him. Although an additional living, that of Coxwold, came to Sterne while he was enjoying his London triumph,[123] writing the novel seems to have shifted his concern from what church preferment would do for him as a man to what it would do for him as a writer. Apparently, he considered that greater preferment would permit greater freedom in writing. He observed that Dean Swift had been able to say things the prebendary could not utter. He too would have freedom after he had been translated with the just.[124] And perhaps it can be said that the novel translated him to another kind of preferment.

What restraints Sterne felt had been imposed upon *Tristram Shandy* make interesting speculation, but the novel gave Sterne a kind of preferment in the church itself. The *Sermons of Mr. Yorick,* made possible by the success of *Tristram Shandy,* reached a desirable congregation and placed him among the Anglican Divines. That Sterne is inferior to Donne, Hall, Taylor, and Tillotson does not so much matter as his being in their company. How Sterne regarded the honor has not been revealed, but he must have been gratified by it. It is admitted that *Tristram Shandy* for many years also made Sterne's ministry suspect, but the twentieth century has begun to view it in a more favorable light.[125]

Neither Sterne nor his public considered him as other than a minister-writer, for it was as such that he was lionized in London

---

[122] Lodwick Hartley, *This Is Lorence*, p. 75.
[123] *Four Portraits*, p. 158.
[124] *Life*, p. 190.
[125] Sterne's *Sermons of Mr. Yorick*, p. 102.

THE NOVEL: TO THE FINAL COMMENT OF YORICK 161

and received in Europe. Part of the scandal of *Tristram Shandy* was also due to the book's having been written by a minister. It was as a minister-writer that Sterne presented Yorick, the hero of the *Sentimental Journey*. Sterne through the agency of his delegated writer Tristram [126] presented in the first volume of *Tristram Shandy* a Yorick who was incapable of expressing himself and was killed by his political enemies.[127] In the second volume Yorick comes again into the novel.[128] Yorick sent a servant to inquire after the sermon the day after Trim and Walter had read it, but Tristram still insists that Yorick is dead. The first and second volumes of *Tristram Shandy* were published January 1, 1760, and again on April 3, 1760. And on May 22, 1760, were published the first two volumes of the *Sermons of Mr. Yorick*.[129] Sterne had prepared the public for the *Sermons* by having his Tristram say that the Shandy family had enough of Yorick's sermons to make a handsome volume. Yorick appears more and more in the succeeding volumes of *Tristram Shandy*. By the end of the novel Yorick is able to make the final statement concerning it. In the *Sentimental Journey*, published after the final volume of *Tristram Shandy*, Yorick exists because he is able to make literary capital out of the most basic elements of his own character, his sentiments.[130]

Yorick had indeed gained preferment and had been translated. Not that Sterne is Yorick, but Sterne came more and more to call himself Yorick. If he can be taken for the Yorick who is developed in the two books, the idealized portrait might be truer than many others that have been made of him. And finally, along with Tristram Shandy's office of translator of the just, Tristram himself should be translated, for without him there scarcely could have been a Yorick.

---

[126] Charles Parish, "A Table of Contents for *Tristram Shandy*", *College English*, X (1960), p. 143.
[127] *Tristram Shandy*, pp. 23-33.
[128] *Ibid.*, pp. 142-143.
[129] *Life*, p. 600.
[130] Ernest Nevin Dilworth, *The Unsentimental Journey of Laurence Sterne* (New York, King's Crown Press, 1948), p. 8.

CONCLUSION

This study of the relationship of *Tristram Shandy* to the life of Sterne has been made on the assumption that a proper evaluation of the novel depends upon whether, or to what degree, it can be regarded as biography or fiction.

The first chapter of the thesis has surveyed the body of the criticism of Sterne and proposed an hypothesis for investigation. Since about 1930 critics have regarded Sterne's novel from a point of view which differs from that of the earlier critics. The earlier ones generally agreed that it was autobiographical. Tristram was Sterne; a book as funny as *Tristram Shandy* was, had been written by a man devoid of serious purposes; and it was useless to look for form in the work of such a writer. The later critics have tended to regard it as a fictional construct, in which Tristram serves as the *persona*. And they have argued cogently for theme in *Tristram Shandy*.

Accordingly, the life and the work have been re-examined. In the second and third chapters of the thesis attention has been focused on the life of the man and of the minister, insofar as they could be separated. In the fourth, it has been shifted from the minister to the novelist and the novel. And in the fifth and sixth, it has remained on the novel.

In the second chapter, after the life of Sterne has been compared with the life of Tristram, the conclusion is reached that neither Tristram nor the other Shandys bear much resemblance to Laurence Sterne or the other members of the author's family, but Parson Yorick appears to be very much like Sterne, the minister. A further conclusion is that Sterne's rearing, education, and reading were partly responsible for *Tristram Shandy's* being other than another jest book.

In the third chapter, from what could be learned of Sterne's training for the ministry and the reading expected of him, from the conventions and practice of preaching, and from what could be observed in Sterne's *Sermons of Mr. Yorick*, the *Letters*, the *Catalogue of Sterne's Library*, and *Tristram Shandy*, it seems reasonable to conclude that the author's twenty years of being a clergyman were highly important in determining the way *Tristram Shandy* was written.

In the fourth chapter we have closely examined in the novel the presentation of Yorick which is set apart from what follows it by two black pages. The conclusion is advanced that Sterne modeled the character of Yorick after his own in order to remove himself from the novel for reasons peculiar to a minister and for which he could have found, and probably did find, precedents. And Yorick was the means by which Sterne not only freed Tristram to write in character but ensured his own distinction from, and participation in, the story.

The fifth chapter has been devoted to examining the first half of the novel and to demonstrating that what Tristram called "the groundwork of the novel" was completed by the middle of the fourth volume. In this stage of the novel Walter Shandy tries to bring into the world a better son than Tristram turns out to be; Tristram tries to present, in the novel he is writing, Walter, Walter's disappointments, and himself as the chief disappointment. Sterne had so well established *Tristram Shandy* as fiction by the middle of the work that it remained primarily and predominantly fiction despite the autobiographical elements which occasionally appeared in the latter half of it.

In the last chapter the entire work is examined and the argument that it is a series, or sequence of events, is advanced. A change in the plan of the work, due to conditions in the life of the author, was made in the second half of the work, and even with the change in plan, Sterne completed the novel in the last chapter of the ninth volume. Attention is directed to the important role of Yorick in the latter part of the work. Yorick, who was removed from *Tristram Shandy* in the first part of it, has been returned to it, made increasingly important to the story, and in the last words of the novel renders a judgment about the kind and quality of the entire work. The final conclusion concerning the relation of *Tristram Shandy* to the life of Sterne is that although the work is fiction, it ultimately reveals, and cannot be separated from, the life of Sterne – the man, the minister, and the novelist.

BIBLIOGRAPHY

PRIMARY SOURCES

The Works of Laurence Sterne, Shakespeare Head Edition, 7 vols. (Oxford, Basil Blackwell, 1926-1927).
A Facsimile Reproduction of a Unique Catalogue of Laurence Sterne's Library, Introduction by Charles Whibley (London, Tregaskis: New York, Wells, 1930).
Letters of Laurence Sterne, Edited by Lewis Perry Curtis (Oxford, Clarendon Press, 1935).
The Life and Opinions of Tristram Shandy, Gentleman (New York, Modern Library, n.d.).
The Life and Opinions of Tristram Shandy, Gent, Edited with notes and introduction by James Aiken Work (New York, Odyssey, 1940).
A Sentimental Journey Through France and Italy, World Classics edition (London, Oxford University Press, 1948).

SECONDARY SOURCES

Abrams, M. H., *The Mirror and the Lamp* (New York, Oxford University Press, 1953).
Allen, Robert J., *The Clubs of Augustan London* (Cambridge, Cambridge University Press, 1933).
Apocrapha, or, Non-Canonical Books of the Bible, The King James Version, Edited by Manuel Komroff (New York, Tudor Publishing Co., 1936).
Arbuthnot, Pope, Swift, Gay, Parnell, Harley, *Memoirs of the Extraordinary Life, Works, and Discoveries of Martinus Scriblerus*, Edited by Charles Kerby-Miller (New Haven, Yale University Press, 1950).
Bacon, Francis, *Advancement of Learning*, Edited by G. W. Kitchins, "Everyman ed." (London and Toronto, J. M. Dent & Sons, 1950).
Bagehot, Walter, "Sterne and Thackeray", in *Literary Studies of Walter Bagehot*, Introduction by George Sampson (London and New York, J. M. Dent and E. P. Dutton, 1911).
✓Baird, Theodore, "The Time-Scheme of *Tristram Shandy* and a Source",

Publications of the Modern Language Association, LI (September, 1936), pp. 803-820.

Baker, Ernest A., *The History of the English Novel*, Vols. III and IV (New York, Barnes and Noble, 1950).

Baldwin, Charles Sears, "The Literary Influence of Sterne in France", *Publications of the Modern Language Association*, X (June, 1902), pp. 221-231.

Becker, Carl L., *The Heavenly City of the Eighteenth-Century Philosophers* (New Haven, Yale University Press, 1932).

Bernbaum, Ernest, *Guide Through the Romantic Movement*, 2d ed. (New York, Ronald Press, 1949).

Booth, Wayne C., "Did Sterne Complete *Tristram Shandy*?", *Modern Philology*, XLVIII (February, 1951), pp. 172-183.

——, "Distance and Point of View", *Essays in Criticism*, XI (January, 1961), pp. 60-79.

——, *The Rhetoric of Fiction* (Chicago, University of Chicago Press, 1961).

——, "The Self-Conscious Narrator in Comic Fiction Before *Tristram Shandy*", *Publications of the Modern Language Association*, LXVII (March, 1952), pp. 163-185.

Boswell, James, *The Life of Samuel Johnson LL.D.*, Edited by George Birveck Hill, revised and enlarged by Laurence F. Powell (Oxford, Clarendon Press), Vols. I-IV (1934); Vols. V-VI (1950).

Boyd, Elizabeth F., *Byron's Don Juan: A Critical Study* (New York, Humanities Press, 1958).

Bredvold, Louis I. (ed.), *Don Juan and Other Satirical Essays* (New York, Odyssey Press, 1935).

Brogan, Howard O., "Fiction and Philosophy in the Education of *Tom Jones, Tristram Shandy*, and *Richard Feveral*", *College English*, XIV (December, 1952), pp. 144-149.

Bullitt, John M., *Jonathan Swift and the Anatomy of Satire* (Cambridge, Harvard University Press, 1953).

Burton, Robert, *Anatomy of Melancholy*, American Reprint of Last London Edition (Philadelphia, J. W. Moore, 1852).

Calder-Marshall, A., "Laurence Sterne", in *The English Novelists: A Survey of the Novel by Twenty Contemporary Novelists*, Edited by Derek Verschoyle (London, Chatto and Windus; New York, Harcourt, Brace & Co., pp. 83-95).

Caldwell, J. R. "The Solemn Romantics", in *Studies in the Comic*, Edited by B. H. Bronson and Others, *University of California Studies in English*, VIII (1914), pp. 251-272.

Carlyle, Thomas, *History of Frederick the Great*, Vol. II (New York, Charles Scribner's Sons, 1903).

——, *Sartor Resartus: The Life and Opinions of Herr Teufelsdröckh*, Edited by Charles Frederick Harrold (New York, Odyssey Press, 1937).

Cash, Arthur, "The Lockean Psychology of *Tristram Shandy*", *A Journal of English Literary History*, XXII (June, 1955), pp. 125-135.

Caskey, J. Homer, "Two Notes on Uncle Toby", *Modern Language Notes*, XVII (May, 1927), pp. 321-323.

Catholic Encyclopedia, 17 vols. (New York, Catholic Encyclopedia Press, 1907-1922).
Cervantes Across the Ages: A Quadricentennial Volume, Edited by Angle Flores and J. M. Berbaditte (New York, The Dryden Press, 1947).
Cervantes Saavedra, Miguel de, *Don Quixote, by Miguel de Cervantes; Ozell's revision of the translation of Peter Motteux*, Introduction by Herschel Brickell (New York, The Modern Library, 1930).
Clark, Edwin, "Sterne's Letters are a Mystery", *New York Times Book Review* (January 15, 1928), pp. 1, 25.
Clifford, James A., and Landa, Louis A. (eds.), *Pope and his Contemporaries: Essays Presented to George Sherburn* (Oxford, The Clarendon Press, 1949).
Coleridge, Samuel Taylor, *Coleridge's Miscellaneous Criticism*, Edited by Thomas Middleton Raysor (London, Constable, 1936).
Connelly, Willard, *Laurence Sterne as Yorick* (London, The Bodley Head, 1958).
Connoly, Cyril, "Sterne and Swift", *Atlantic Monthly*, CLXXV (June, 1945), pp. 94-96.
Cook, Albert, "Reflexive Attitudes: Sterne, Gogol, Gide", *Criticism*, II (Spring, 1960), pp. 164-174.
Cordasco, Francesco, *Laurence Sterne: A List of Critical Studies Published from 1896 to 1946* (Brooklyn, Long Island University Press, 1948).
Cowper, William, *Correspondence of William Cowper*, Edited by Thomas Wright, 4 vols. (London, Hodder and Stoughton, 1904).
Crane, Ronald S., "The Concept of Plot and the Plot of 'Tom Jones' ", in *Critics and Criticism* (Chicago, The University of Chicago Press, 1952).
Cross, Wilbur L., *The Development of the English Novel* (New York, Macmillan, 1923).
——, *The Life and Times of Laurence Sterne*, New edition (New Haven, Yale University Press, 1925).
Cubberly, Edward P., *History of Education* (New York, Macmillan Co., 1920).
Curtis, Lewis P., "Forged Letters of Laurence Sterne", *Publications of the Modern Language Association*, L (December, 1935), pp. 1076-1106.
——, (ed.), *Letters of Laurence Sterne* (Oxford, The Clarendon Press, 1935).
——, "New Light on Sterne", *Modern Language Notes*, LXXVI (June, 1961), pp. 498-501.
Dampier, William Cecil, *A History of Science and its Relation with Philosophy and Religion*, 4th ed. (Cambridge, Cambridge University Press, 1949).
De Voto, Bernard, *The World of Fiction* (Boston, Houghton Mifflin Co., 1950).
Dictionary of the Bible, Edited by James Hastings (New York, Charles Scribner's Sons, 1947).
Dilworth, Ernest Nevin, *The Unsentimental Journey of Laurence Sterne* (New York, The King's Crown Press, 1948).
——, "Sterne: Some Devices", *Notes and Queries*, New Series, CXCVII (1952), pp. 165-166.

Eddy, William A., "Tom Brown and *Tristram Shandy*", *Modern Language Notes*, XLIV (June, 1929), pp. 379-381.
Eighteenth Century Poetry and Prose. 2d ed., edited by Louis I. Bredvold, A. D. McKillop, and Lois Whitney (New York, Ronald Press Co., 1956).
Eliot, T. S., *Selected Essays 1817-1932* (New York, Harcourt, Brace and Co., 1932).
Encyclopedia of Religion and Ethics, Edited by James Hastings, 12 vols. (New York, Charles Scribner's Sons, 1914).
Essays Catholic and Critical, Edited by Edward Gordon Selwyn (New York and Toronto, Macmillan Co., 1926).
Evans, A. W., *Warburton and the Warburtonians: a Study in Some Eighteenth Century Controversies* (Oxford, Oxford University Press, 1932).
Faulkner, William, *The Faulkner Reader: Selections from the Works of William Faulkner* (New York, Random House, 1954).
Ferriar, John, *Illustrations of Sterne: With Other Essays and Verses*, 2 vols. (London, Printed in Manchester, 1798).
———, *Illustrations of Sterne: With Other Essays and Verses*, 2d ed. revised, 2 vols. (London, Cadell and Davies, 1812).
Fitzgerald, Percy, *The Life of Laurence Sterne*, 2 vols. (London, Downey, 1896).
Forster, Edward Morgan, *Aspects of the Novel* (New York, Harcourt, Brace and Co., 1927).
Fredman, Alice Green, *Diderot and Sterne* (New York, Columbia University Press, 1955).
Frye, Northrop, *Anatomy of Criticism* (Princeton, Princeton University Press, 1947).
———, "Towards Defining an Age of Sensibility", *Journal of English Literary History*, XXIII (June, 1956), pp. 144-152.
Gibson, Walker, "Authors, Speakers, Readers, and Mock Readers", *College English*, XI (February, 1950), pp. 265-269.
Gray, Thomas, *Correspondence of Thomas Gray*, Edited by Paget Toynbee and Whibley, Leonard, 3 vols. (Oxford, The Clarendon Press, 1935).
Greenberg, Bernard L., "Laurence Sterne and Chambers' 'Encyclopedia' ", *Modern Language Notes*, LXIX (December, 1954), pp. 560-562.
Greene, Graham, "Fielding and Sterne", in *From Anne to Victoria: Essays by Various Hands*, Edited by Bonamy Dobree (New York, Scribner's, 1937), pp. 279-289.
———, *The Lost Childhood* (London, Eyre and Spottiswoode, 1951).
Hammond, Lansing Van der Heyden, *Laurence Sterne's "Sermons of Mr. Yorick"* (New Haven, Yale University Press, 1948).
Harper, Kenneth, "A Russian Critic and *Tristram Shandy*", *Modern Philology*, LII (November, 1954), pp. 92-99.
Hartley, Lodwick, *This is Lorence* (Chapel Hill, The University of North Carolina Press, 1943).
Hazlitt, William, *William Hazlitt: Complete Works*, Edited by P. P. Howes, "Centenary ed." (London and Toronto, J. M. Dent, 1930-1934).
———, "Tristram and the Angel", *College English*, IX (November, 1947), pp. 62-69.
Hermes Trismégiste, Fragments Extraits de Stobée, texte établi et traduit

BIBLIOGRAPHY

A. J. Festugiere, "Société l'édition" (Paris, Les Belles Lettres, 1954).
Herodotus, *The Persian Wars*, Translated by George Rawlinson (New York, Modern Library, 1947).
Holbrook, Jackson, *Great English Novelists* (London, G. Richards, 1908).
Holland, Norman N., "The Laughter of Laurence Sterne", *Hudson Review*, IX (Autumn, 1956), pp. 422-430.
Hooker, Edward Niles, "The Discussion of Taste, from 1750 to 1770, and the New Trends in Literary Criticism", *Publications of the Modern Language Association*, XLIX (June, 1934), pp. 577-592.
——, "The Reviewers and the New Criticism", *Philological Quarterly*, XIII (April, 1934), pp. 189-202.
Howes, Alan B., *Yorick and the Critics: Sterne's Reputation in England, 1760-1868* (New Haven, Yale University Press, 1958).
Hughes, Helen Sard, "A Precursor of *Tristram Shandy*", *Journal of English and Germanic Philology*, XVII (April, 1918), pp. 227-251.
Humphrey, Robert, *Stream of Consciousness in the Modern Novel* (Berkeley and Los Angeles, University of California Press, 1954).
James, Henry, *The Art of the Novel: Critical Prefaces* (New York, Charles Scribner's Sons, 1934).
Jefferson, D. W., "*Tristram Shandy* and its Tradition", in *From Dryden to Johnson: The Pelican Guide to English Literature* (Hormondsworth, Middlesex, Penguin Books, Ltd., 1957).
✓——, "Tristram Shandy and the Tradition of Learned Wit", *Essays in Criticism*, I (July, 1951), pp. 225-248.
Johnson's England, 2 vols. Edited by A. S. Tuberville (Oxford, The Clarendon Press, 1933).
Johnson, Samuel, *Works*, "Library Club edition" (Troy, N. Y., Pafreats Book Co., 1903).
Jones, Richard F., *Ancients and Moderns: A Study of the Background of the Battle of the Books* (= *Washington University Studies in Language and Literature*, No. 6) (St. Louis, Mo., Washington University Press, 1936).
Jones, Richard F., "The Background of the Attack on Science in the Age of Pope", in *Pope and his Contemporaries: Essays Presented to George Sherburn* (Oxford, The Clarendon Press, 1949).
Kettle, Arnold, *An Introduction to the English Novel* (London, Hutchinson's, 1951-1953).
✓Krutch, Joseph Wood, *Five Masters: A Study in the Mutations of the Novel* (Bloomington, Indiana University Press, 1959).
✓Laird, John, "Shandean Philosophy", in *Philosophical Incursions into English Literature* (Cambridge, Cambridge University Press, 1946), pp. 74-91.
Leavis, Frank R., *The Great Tradition*, "Doubleday Anchor Book" (New York, Doubleday, 1954).
Lecky, W. E. C., *History of the Rise and Influence of the Spirit of Rationalism in Europe*, Edited by C. Wright Mills (New York, George Braziliert, 1955).
Lee, Sidney, "Laurence Sterne", in *Dictionary of National Biography*, Edited by Leslie Stephen and Sidney Lee (New York, Oxford University Press, 1921-1922), XVIII, pp. 1086-1110.

Lehman, B. H., "Comedy and Laughter", in *Five Gayley Lectures* (Berkeley and Los Angeles, University of Califorina Press, 1954).

——, "Of Time, Personality, and the Author", in *Studies in the Comic, University of California Studies in English*, VII (1941), pp. 233-250.

Literary History of England, Edited by Albert C. Baugh and Others (New York, Appleton-Century-Crofts, 1948).

Locke, John, *An Essay Concerning Human Understanding*, Edited by Alexander Campbell Fraser, 2 vols. (Oxford, The Clarendon Press, 1894).

——, *Two Treatises of Government: A Critical Edition with an Introduction and Apparatus Criticus by Peter Laslett* (Cambridge, Cambridge University Press, 1960).

——, *Two Treatises of Government. With a supplement, Patriarcha*, Edited with an Introduction by Thomas I. Cook (New York, Hofner Publishing Co., 1947).

Lubbock, Percy, *The Craft of Fiction* (New York, P. Smith, 1945).

Lussky, Alfred Edwin, *Tieck's Romantic Irony With Special Emphasis upon the Influence of Cervantes, Sterne, and Goethe* (Chapel Hill, University of North Carolina Press, 1932).

Mack, Maynard (ed.), *The Augustans*, Vol. V of *English Masterpieces* (New York, Prentice-Hall, Inc., 1950).

MacLean, Kenneth, "English Literature, 1660-1800", in *Philological Quarterly*, XXXIV (July, 1955), p. 314.

——, "Imagination and Sympathy: Sterne and Adam Smith", *Journal of the History of Ideas*, X (June, 1949), pp. 399-410.

——, "The Imagination in *Tristram Shandy*", *Explorations*, III (August, 1954), pp. 59-64.

——, *John Locke and English Literature of the Eighteenth Century* (New Haven, Yale University Press, 1936).

McCullough, Bruce Walker, *Representative English Novelists: DeFoe to Conrad* (New York, Harper, 1946), pp. 71-83.

McKillop, Allan Dugals, *The Early Masters of the English Fiction* (Lawrence, Kansas, The University of Kansas Press, 1956), pp. 185-214.

——, "Laurence Sterne", *English Literature from Dryden to Burns* (New York, Appleton-Century-Crofts, 1948).

Mendilow, Adam Abraham, *Time and the Novel* (London, P. Nevill, 1952).

Merwin, Henry Childs, "The Philosophy of Sterne", *Atlantic Monthly*, LXXIV (October, 1894), pp. 521-527.

Meyers, Walter L., "O, the Hobby Horse", *Virginia Quarterly Review*, XIX (Spring, 1943), pp. 268-277.

Mitchell, W. Fraser, *English Pulpit Oratory from Andrews to Tillotson* (London, S.P.C.K., 1932).

Monro, D. H., *Argument of Laughter* (Melbourne, Melbourne University Press, 1951).

Montaigne, Michel, *The Essays of Michel Eyquem de Montaigne*, Translated by Charles Cotton, Edited by W. Carew Hazlitt, In *Great Books of the Western World* (Chicago, London; Toronto, Encyclopedia Britannica, Inc., 1952).

Muir, Edwin, *The Structure of the Novel* (London, Hogarth Press, 1928).

Munroe, Paul, *A Text-Book of the History of Education* (New York, MacMillan Co., 1938).
Murray, Sir J. A. H., *Oxford English Dictionary* (Oxford, The Clarendon Press, 1933).
Ollard, S. L., "Sterne as a Parish Priest", *Times Literary Supplement*, May 25, 1933, and June 1, 1933.
Oxford Companion to English Literature, Edited by Paul Harvey. 3d ed. (Oxford, The Clarendon Press, 1946).
Parish, Charles, "A Table of Contents for Tristram Shandy", *College English*, X (December, 1960), pp. 143-150.
——, "Twentieth-Century Criticism of Form in *Tristram Shandy*", Unpublished Ph.D. dissertation, University of New Mexico (1959).
Piper, William Bowen, "Tristram Shandy's Tragicomical Testimony", *Criticism*, III (Summer, 1961).
Powys, Llewelyn, "Laurence Sterne", *Bookman*, LVIII (September, 1923), pp. 10-16.
Pritchett, V. S., "Defoe", in *The English Novelists*, Edited by Derek Verschoyle (London, Chatto and Windus, 1936).
Preistly, John B., "The Brothers Shandy", in *The English Comic Characters* (London, J. Lane, 1928).
Puffendorf [Samuel], *Of the Law of Nature and of Nations*, 8 books; 4th ed. (London, J. Walthoe and Others, 1729).
Putney, Rufus D., "Alas Poor Eliza", *Modern Language Review*, XLI (October, 1946), pp. 411-413.
——, "Laurence Sterne, Apostle of Laughter", in *The Age of Johnson: Essays Presented to Chauncey Brewster Tinker* (New Haven, Yale University Press), pp. 159-170.
——, "The Evolution of a Sentimental Journey", *Philological Quarterly*, XIX (October, 1940), pp. 349-369.
Quennell, Peter, *Four Portraits* (London, William Collins, 1945). In the U.S. *The Profane Virtues* (New York, Viking Press, 1945).
Rabelais, François, *Gargantua and Pantagruel* (New York, Dodd, Mead & Co., n.d.).
Raleigh, Sir Walter Alexander, *The English Novel* (London, John Murray, 1911).
Rawson, C. J., " 'Tristram Shandy' and 'Candide' ", *Notes and Queries*, May, 1958, p. 226.
Read, Herbert, *English Prose Style* (London, A. Bell & Sons, 1949).
——, *English Prose Style* (New York, Henry Holt & Co., 1928).
——, "Sterne", in *The Sense of Glory* (New York, Harcourt, Brace and Co., 1930).
Reid, Ben, "The Sad Hilarity of Sterne", *Virginia Quarterly Review*, XXXII (Winter, 1956), pp. 107-130.
Roberts, S. C., *A History of the Cambridge University Press, 1521-1921* (Cambridge, Cambridge University Press, 1921).
Robinson, F. N., *The Poetical Works of Chaucer*, "Cambridge ed." (Boston, Houghton Mifflin Co., 1933).
Russel, H. K., "*Tristram Shandy* and the Technique of the Novel", *Studies in Philology*, XLII (July, 1945), pp. 581-593.

Sallé, Jean-Cloud, "A Source of Sterne's Conception of Time", *Review of English Studies*, VI (April, 1955), pp. 180-182.

St. Augustine, *Basic Writings of Saint Augustine*, Edited by Whitney J. Oates, 2 vols. (New York, Random House, 1948).

St. Thomas, *Basic Writings of St. Thomas*, Edited by Anton C. Pegis (New York, Random House, 1944).

Scott, Walter, *The Novels of Sterne, Goldsmith, Dr. Johnson, Mackenzie, Horace Walpole, and Clara Reeve, to which are Prefixed, Memoirs of the Lives of the Authors*. "Ballantine's Novelist's Library", Vol. V (London, Hurst, Robinson, and Co., 1823).

Seidlin, Oscar, "Laurence Sterne's *Tristram Shandy* and Thomas Mann's *Joseph, the Provider*", *Modern Language Quarterly*, VIII (June, 1947), pp. 101-118.

A Select of Nicene and Post-Nicene Fathers of the Christian Church, Second Series, Edited by Philip Schaff, Henry Wace and Others, 14 vols. (Grand Rapids, Michigan, W. B. Eerdmans, 1952-1956).

Seligmann, Kurt, *The History of Magic* (New York, Pantheon Books, 1948).

Shaw, Margaret R. B., *The Making of a Humorist* (London, Richards Press, 1957).

Shepperson, Archibald B., *The Novel in Motley: A History of the Burlesque in English* (Cambridge, Harvard University Press, 1936).

——, "Yorick as Ministering Angel", *Virginia Quarterly Review*, XXX (Winter, 1954), pp. 54-56.

Sherman, Stuart, "Laurence Sterne: A Graceless Man of God", in *Critical Woodcuts* (New York, Charles Scribner's Sons, 1926).

Sherwood, Irma Z., "The Novelists as Commentators", in *The Age of Johnson* (New Haven, Yale University Press, 1949), pp. 113-126.

Shine, Hill, *Carlyle's Early Reading to 1834*, "Occasional Contribution, No. 57" (Lexington, University of Kentucky Libraries, 1953).

Sichel, Walter Sydney, *Sterne: A Study: to which is added the Journal to Eliza* (Philadelphia, Lippincott, 1910).

The Spectator, Edited by Gregory Smith, 4 vols., "Everyman's Library" (London, J. M. Dent & Sons, 1933).

Stauffer, Donald A., *The Art of Biography in Eighteenth Century England* (Princeton, Princeton University Press, 1941).

Stedmond, J. M., "Genre and *Tristram Shandy*", *Philological Quarterly*, XXXVIII (January, 1959), pp. 37-51.

Stephen, Leslie, *The History of English Thought in the Eighteenth Century*, 3d ed., 2 vols. (New York, Putnam's, 1927).

Sterne, Laurence, *A Sentimental Journey*, Introduction by Virginia Woolf (London, Oxford University Press, n.d.).

Swift, Jonathan, *Gulliver's Travels*, Edited by Herbert Davis, with an Introduction by Harold Williams (Oxford, Basil Blackwell, 1959).

——, *A Tale of a Tub to which is added the battle of the books and the Mechanical operation of the spirit*, Edited by A. C. Guthkelch and D. N. Smith (Oxford, The Clarendon Press, 1920).

Thayer, Harvey Waterman, *Laurence Sterne in Germany* (New York, Columbia University Press, 1905).

Thompson, J. A. K., *Irony: An Historical Introduction* (Cambridge, Harvard University Press, 1927).
Thucydides, *The Complete Writings of Thucydides: The Peloponnesian War*, The unabridged Crawley translation (New York, The Modern Library, 1934).
Tindall, William York, *The Literary Symbol* (Bloomington, Indiana University Press, 1955).
Tobin, James E., *Eighteenth Century English Literature and Its Cultural Background. A Bibliography* (New York, Fordham University Press, 1939).
Tomkins, J. M. S., "Triglyph and Tristram", *Times Literary Supplement*, July 11, 1929.
Towers, A. R., "Sterne's Cock and Bull Story", *Journal of English Literary History*, XXIV (March, 1957), pp. 12-29.
Traill, H. D., *Sterne*, "English Men of Letters" (New York, MacMillan Co., 1902).
Traugott, John, *Tristram Shandy's World, Sterne's Philosophical Rhetoric* (Berkeley, University of California Press, 1954).
Trevelyan, George Macaulay, *A Shortened History of England* (London, New York, and Toronto, Longmans, Greene & Co., 1942).
Tuberville, A. S., *English Men and Manners of the Eighteenth Century* (Galaxy Books, New York, Oxford University Press).
Turnbull, John M., "The Prototype of Walter Shandy's Tristrapaedia", *Review of English Studies*, LXXIII (April, 1926), pp. 212-215.
Van Ghent, Dorothy, *The English Novel: Form and Structure* (New York, Rinehart, 1953), pp. 83-98.
Vaughn, C. E., "Sterne and the Novel of his Times", in *The Cambridge History of English Literature*, Vol. X.
Warburton, William, *The Divine Legation of Moses*, 2d ed. (London, Printed for the Executor of the late Mr. Giles Fletcher, 1742).
Wasserman, Earl R., "Byron and Sterne", *Modern Language Notes*, LXX (January, 1955), p. 25.
Watkins, Walter Barker Critz, *Perilous Balance* (Princeton, Princeton University Press, 1939).
Watson, Wilfred, "The Fifth Commandment: Some Allusions to Sir Robert Filmer's Writings in *Tristram Shandy*", *Modern Language Notes*, LXII (April, 1947), pp. 234-240.
Watt, Ian, *The Rise of the Novel: Studies in Defoe, Richardson, & Fielding* (London, Chatto and Windus, University of California Press, 1957).
Wellek, René, and Warren, Austin, *Theory of Literature* (New York, Harcourt, Brace and Co., 1942).
Weston, Jessie L., *From Ritual to Romance* (Garden City, New York, Doubleday Anchor Books, 1957).
Whitehead, Alfred North, *Symbolism* (Cambridge, Cambridge University Press).
Willey, Basil, *The Eighteenth Century Background* (New York, Columbia University Press, 1952).
——, *The Seventeenth Century Background* (New York, Doubleday & Co., 1955).

Wimsatt, William K., and Brooks, Cleanth, *Literary Criticism: A Short History* (New York, Alfred A. Knopf, 1957).
Winstanley, D. A., *The University of Cambridge in the Eighteenth Century* (Cambridge, Cambridge University Press, 1922).
Worcester, David, *The Art of Satire* (Cambridge, Mass., Harvard University Press, 1940).
Work, James (ed.), *Tristram Shandy* (New York, Odyssey Press, 1940).
Works of Lord Byron: Poetry, Edited by E. H. Coleridge (London and New York, J. Murray and Scribner's, 1898-1904).
Works of Lord Byron: Prose, Edited by Roland E. Prothero (London and New York, J. Murray and Scribner's, 1898-1904).
Wright, Nathalia, *Melville's Use of the Bible* (Durham, North Carolina, Duke University Press, 1949).
Yoseloff, Thomas, *A Fellow of Infinite Jest* (New York, Prentice-Hall, Inc., 1945).
Zabel, Morton D., *Literary Opinion in America* (New York, Harper & Brothers, 1951).

STUDIES IN ENGLISH LITERATURE

1. WILLIAM H. MATCHETT: *The Phoenix and the Turtle: Shakespeare's Poem and Chester's Loues Martyr.* 1965. 213 pp. Cloth. Gld. 26.—

2. RONALD DAVID EMMA: *Milton's Grammar.* 1964. 164 pp. Gld. 18.—

3. GEORGE A. PANICHAS: *Adventure in Consciousness: The Meaning of D. H. Lawrence's Religious Quest.* 1964. 225 pp., portrait. Gld. 25.—

4. HENRIETTA TEN HARMSEL: *Jane Austen: A Study in Fictional Conventions.* 1964. 206 pp. Gld. 25.—

5. DOROTHY SCHUCHMAN MCCOY: *Tradition and Convention: A Study of Periphrasis in English Pastoral Poetry from 1556-1715.* 1965. 289 pp. Gld. 30.—

6. TED E. BOYLE: *Symbol and Meaning in the Fiction of Joseph Conrad.* 1965. 245 pp. Gld. 24.—

7. JOSEPHINE O'BRIEN SCHAEFER: *The Three-Fold Nature of Reality of the Novels of Virginia Woolf.* 1965. 210 pp. Gld. 24.—

8. GERARD ANTHONY PILECKI: *Shaw's "Geneva": A Critical Study of the Evolution of the Text in Relation to Shaw's Political Thought and Dramatic Practice.* 1965. 189 pp. Gld. 20.—

9. BLAZE ODELL BONAZZA: *Shakespeare's Early Comedies: A Structural Analysis.* 1966. 125 pp. Cloth. Gld. 18.—

10. THOMAS KRANIDAS: *The Fierce Equation: A Study of Milton's Decorum.* 1965. 165 pp. Cloth. Gld. 21.—

11. KENNETH HUGH BYRON: *The Pessimism of James Thomson (B.V.) in Relation to his Times.* 1965. 174 pp. Cloth. Gld. 20.—

12. ROLAND A. DUERKSEN: *Shelleyan Ideas in Victorian Literature.* 1966. 208 pp. Cloth. Gld. 24.—

16. BARBARA BARTHOLOMEW: *Fortuna and Natura: A Reading of Three Chaucer Narratives.* 1966. 112 pp. Cloth.   Gld. 17.—

17. GEORG B. FERGUSON: *John Fletcher: The Woman's Prize or The Tamer Tamed. A Critical Edition.* 1966. 223 pp. Cloth.
Gld. 24.—

18. EDWARD VASTA: *The Spiritual Basis of "Piers Plowman".* 1965. 143 pp. Cloth.   Gld. 18.—

19. WILLIAM B. TOOLE: *Shakespeare's Problem Plays: Studies in Form and Meaning.* 1966. 242 pp. Cloth.   Gld. 28.—

25. WILLIAM M. WIJNKOOP: *Three Children of the Universe: Emerson's View of Shakespeare, Bacon, and Milton.* 1966. 199 pp., portrait. Cloth.   Gld. 22.—

MOUTON & CO. — PUBLISHERS — THE HAGUE

10-30-67 JLC

10-30-67 JLC